P. F. Parisot

The Reminiscences of a Texas Missionary

P. F. Parisot

The Reminiscences of a Texas Missionary

ISBN/EAN: 9783744653114

Printed in Europe, USA, Canada, Australia, Japan

Cover: Foto ©ninafisch / pixelio.de

More available books at **www.hansebooks.com**

THE
REMINISCENCES
OF A
Texas Missionary.

BY

REV. P. F. PARISOT, O. M. I.

ST. MARY'S CHURCH
SAN ANTONIO, TEXAS.
1899.

PRESS OF
JOHNSON BROS. PRINTING CO
SAN ANTONIO, TEXAS

SAN ANTONIO, TEXAS, JAN. 22, 1899.

We cordially encourage the publication and circulation of the "Reminiscences of a Texas Missionary" by the Rev. P. F. Parisot, O. M. I.

† JOHN A. FOREST,
Bishop of San Antonio.

SAN ANTONIO, TEXAS, JAN. 12, 1899.

We have authorized the publication of the book entitled 'Reminiscences of a Texas Missionary" written by the Rev. P. F. Parisot, O. M. I.

JOSEPH LEFEBVRE, O. M. I.
Provincial.

NEW ORLEANS, LA., DEC. 5, 1896.

"The Reminiscences of a Texas Missionary" are very interesting. I keep a clip-book for the history of the diocese principally, and would like to have the whole series.

† F. JANSSENS,
Archbishop of New Orleans.

The Right Reverend P. J. Hurth, of Dacca, Bengal, India, formerly President of St. Edward's College, Austin, Texas, writes:

"I readily recognized the venerable Father Parisot in the 'Reminiscences of a Texas Missionary,' which are very interesting, and which will always remain good reading for the young clergy.

† P. J. HURTH,
Bishop of Dacca."

COPYRIGHT 1899,
BY
REV. P. F. PARISOT, O. M. I.

PART I.
TEXAS AND LOUISIANA.
CHAPTER I.

1852. Adieu to Belle France. Aspect of the Diocese of Galveston. My first trip. Penniless. General Chambers. Liberty. Sour Lake. Prayer answered. Two nights in a box. Back to Galveston. Yellow Jack. Second Mission tour. Raw Sweet potato for my supper. Jasper.

In the month of March, 1852, six Oblate Fathers and one Lay Brother, accompanied by four Nuns of the Incarnate Word, two Ursuline Sisters, four Brothers of Mary, and eighteen Seminarians, bade adieu to "La Belle France" and went aboard the sailing vessel "La Belle Assise," at Havre, en route for Texas.

"My native land adieu! adieu!
I cannot always stay with you, stay with you."

The wharf is crowded, thousands are there, in expectation of an unwonted spectacle. The saintly Bishop Odin, in his episcopal robes, blesses the band of missionaries from the pier and then goes back to Paris, in the interest of his diocese. The ship leaves its moorings, the cannon booms, the Ave Maris Stella is sung by thirty-five voices. "Adieu ma belle France." The sacrifice is made joyfully, "Hilarem datorem diligit Deus." Some sing, "Partons pour la Syrie." I saw tears trickling down the cheeks of a tender-hearted seminarian, as he cast a last glance on the coast of France disappearing on the horizon. "Adieu, mother."

Fifty-two days between the immensity of the firmament and the immensity of the ocean taught us to appreciate the fixity of mother earth. New Orleans at last. The seminarians go to Barrens, Missouri, to finish their ecclesiastical studies. The rest go to Galveston, a city of 6,000 souls. Here we find the episcopal residence, a rather poor-looking place, a frame house with six or seven rooms. The occupants were the Very Rev. Chambodut, V. G., and Rev. M. Huc.

At that time there were in the whole State of Texas, the following Priests: the Rev. Clark at Houston, the Rev. Miller at Brazoria, the Rev. Anstaett at Victoria, the Rev. Padey at Refugio, the Rev. Dubuis at San Antonio, the Rev. Giraudon at Laredo, the Rev. Borrajo at Eagle Pass. In all nine Priests for the whole diocese of Texas. In the course of a year this number was increased by the Revs. Dixon, Heggarty O'Reilly, Sheehan, O'Driscoll and six Oblate Fathers.

In the month of February, 1853, I was sent by Bishop Odin to visit Eastern Texas. I had just $2.00 in my pocket and a heavy saddle-bag, containing all articles necessary for the Mass and my wardrobe. I went on board a steamer, crossed over Galveston Bay, paid my fare, $2.00, and landed at Chambersville penniless. I entered the town, which contained three houses, the most conspicuous of which was General Chambers' residence. I directed my steps thereto, with my heavy saddle-bag on my shoulders, and met General Chambers on the door steps. "Good morning, General," said I, "I am sent by Bishop Odin to visit Eastern Texas. I have no horse, no money, and do not know the roads. Can you help me out?"

"How can your Bishop send you without money? Go back to Galveston by return boat, I shall pay your fare. You must come back better equipped."

"Much obliged to you, General, I think I will take my saddle-bag on my shoulders and go ahead." The

General, seeing my obstinacy, lent me a big American horse and a colored man to accompany me. We reached a settlement six miles ahead, called Turtle Bayou, where I sojourned three days. Here they lent me a donkey. It took me the whole day to reach the next settlement, fifteen miles distant. Here I prepared for First Communion a sick girl, who died a few days afterwards. I reached Liberty, where twenty-five children made their First Communion, after an eight days' preparation. En route for Beaumont, half way, where the road forks to the left, I saw a board stuck in the mud bearing the following inscription, "Sour Lake." Led by mere curiosity I went to see the lake. On arriving, a gentleman asked me if I were a Catholic Priest, and on my answering affirmatively, he invited me to see a dying lady, who had been praying to Almighty God to send her a priest.

The following day I said mass in her room and administered the last Sacraments, blessing God, who made me quit the high road through curiosity. She died shortly after.

At Beaumont, I could not find a single Catholic; so I went a few miles below, where lived a Mr. Chiasson, with his numerous family and his father, aged 103 years, who was as deaf as a post. I had to hear the old man's confession half a mile from the house behind a bush. After a few days spent in that neighborhood I started for Orange, where I met an Alsatian, who had arrived there a few days previous. He was the only Catholic in the place. He had for a dwelling place a kind of hut, or rather a box six feet cube, where we both slept comfortably, after partaking of a supper, prepared in a small tin plate over a lamp.

The following day being Sunday, I was shown a house where a German lady lived, supposed to be a

Catholic. Here I said Mass. The whole place was out just to see the Priest; but all behaved very well during Mass.

Out of ten settlements I visited, this was the only place, where I did not administer a single baptism. After calling with all my heart the blessing of God upon the man in the box, I left the place and went back to Galveston. The Alsatian, who tendered me his hut for two days and two nights, came to see me in Galveston in 1856. He was dressed as a gentleman, and bore the title of Captain. He had come from Orange on a schooner loaded with lumber. "The schooner," he said, "is mine, the cargo is mine, and the box six feet cube is now a chicken coop in my yard. I have now a two-story house. Come and see me, and we shall chat on the vicissitudes of human affairs."

After this, my first trip, I became convinced, that my knowledge of English was very limited, so I sat down to review my grammar.

Alas! alas! O woful year 1853! The angel of death accompanied with the dread plague of yellow fever, came hovering over Galveston, claiming 300 victims, among whom were five Priests, Rev. Fathers Dixon; Baudrand, O. M. I., Huc, O'Driscoll, Metton, and a subdeacon, Rev. Bajar, all lately arrived.

The Vicar General and two Oblate Fathers were spared.

The doctors advised the Priests, who were not necessary for the ministry, to leave town and go to the interior of the State. They answered that they would rather die, than leave the post of peril and be looked upon as cowards.

A protestant lady, inquiring who were buried in these freshly opened graves in front of the Cathedral, was told that they contained six Catholic clergymen who had died of yellow fever. "Why did they not leave the place," said she, "and save their lives as our minister did?" "Their duty compelled them to stay and die, was the answer."

The lady shed tears of compassion on the graves of these martyrs of duty. It was ascertained afterwards that she joined the Catholic Church.

The Catholic population of Texas at this time (1853) was about 20,000. The number of Priests employed on the mission was tripled since 1852. A new impetus was given to missionary work. The Brothers of Mary had opened their college at San Antonio under favorable auspices. The Sisters of the Incarnate Word, lodged in a private residence at Brownsville, impatiently waited for the completion of their convent then in course of erection, and employed their time in teaching a few girls from Brownsville and Matamoros, Mex. Three Oblate Fathers, with a lay Brother, commenced work on the lower Rio Grande, visiting the ranches along the road to Corpus Christi, and those scattered on the banks of the river as far as Roma. Resident Priests were stationed at some of the principal posts. But Eastern Texas was still a foreign mission, and I was the missionary "in partibus infidelium."

After recuperating from a serious attack of yellow fever I was again sent to visit those places in Texas, which had not been visited by any Priest for a number of years. This time I was out for nearly three months.

The first settlement I visited was situated on the right side of Trinity river. When I arrived at the crossing, the ferry-boat was on the opposite side of the river, and there was no one to take me over. For fully one hour I hallooed for the ferryman at the highest pitch of my voice, until I became hoarse. In my distress, I got astride on two logs tied together and crossed the river, paddling with my hands. I brought the ferry-boat over, but being carried some distance below by the current, it took me a long time to return. Now to ferry my horse over. Here was the rub. On arriving on the opposite bank the water was so shallow that I had to jump into it and push the boat until I was saturated with water and prespiration. When I arrived at the house of the ferryman he was amazed at the recital of my manoeuvre, and could not understand how I managed to get over the river and cross with the heavy ferry-boat, alone. Finally, I arrived at the settlement and commenced work. An old man came from his farm, situated a short distance from the settlement, to see me. He had obtained a grant of 640 acres of land from the Mexican Government years before. A proviso of the law was that a man with a family could obtain the grant, provided he was a Catholic. This man had been influenced by human motives to become a Catholic, but was very ignorant of the tenets of the Church. Upon asking me if I could forgive his sins, "Yes Sir," I told him, "if you confess them with sorrow, for the Priests are the ambassadors of Christ, the dispensers of the mysteries of God, to whom Christ said, " Whose sins you shall forgive, they are forgiven them, &c." But the poor man would not submit and confess, and went out sorrowful. He had not entered the fold of Christ by the right door, or at least, with the right intention. After I had finished my mission at that place, I was advised to return by water. The river had of late overflowed and left plently of water in the swamps. The people furnished me with a boat and a colored man, but in some places the water was so shallow that we had to wade and push the boat through the mud. Sometimes wo were caught between two trees. To make the story short we made nine miles in twelve hours. After recrossing the Trinity river it was after 9 o'clock p. m, There was a house close by on the bank of the river. Entering, I asked the occupants to allow me to stay there until about midnight, in order to recite my Breviary. They had neither lamp nor candle, so they made a fire to enable me to read my office. At the conclusion I asked the people, if they had anything to eat. They said they had nothing but raw sweet potatoes. I put one on the fire, and ate it half cooked, swallowing the last mouthful a few minutes before midnight. We bade the people good night and going up the river one mile, tied our boat, and reached a settlement three miles from the river, where I said Mass at 10 o'clock. Starting from that place, I passed through Liberty, where I stopped one day to recuperate. I was furnished with a mare accompanied by her colt, to take me to a Mr. Hardin's, living some miles above Liberty. I got lost in the woods, but after rambling to the right and left for five hours, I arrived at 10 p. m. at Mr. Hardin's place. The gentleman received me very kindly, preparing my cold supper himself.

The next day I said Mass for his three daughters, who had joined the Catholic Church in Galveston, while attending school at the Ursuline Convent.

After breakfast Mr. Hardin lent me a good horse to carry me to a place fifteen miles farther on. There I bought an old jade for $20, all the money I had in my purse. One day wanting to cross over the river Neches, I told the ferryman to choose between prayer and preaching, for I had no money with me. "Well, pray for my family," he said, and invited me to take dinner with him. The following day I reached Jasper, and met there a good Irishman, who was then working as a carpenter, in the construction of a court house. "I am." he said, "the only Catholic in the place, but one mile from here lives another Irishman with a numerous family." The next day early in the morning, the whole place was astir, anxious to see the Priest. Many had not heretofore seen a Catholic Priest. I said Mass under the gallery in front of the Irishman's house. The greater part of my audience were standing in the yard, some of them being disappointed to see that the Priest was just like any other man.

After crossing the Sabine river, I visited Calcasieu Parish, an immense district in Louisiana, in some parts of which a Priest had not been seen for fifteen or twenty years. After having visited a few localities my old jade refused to carry me any farther. I said good-bye to the poor beast and bought a mustang, a wild horse that had been caught a few days previous in the prairie and was not "broken" as they say in that country.

CHAPTER II.

Calcasieu. My Mustang. Mary comes to my Rescue. Lost in the Pine-wood. In the nick of time. Laudanum did it. Drowned girl swallowed by an Alligator. Cow Boys. How I crossed bayous. From Mensa Episcopali to a kitchen. Third Trip. Fifty baptisms in a small Settlement. Rivers Calcasieu and Mermenteau Indians.

This first visit to Calcasieu was filled with many unpleasant episodes, but with great inward consolations in the discharge of my ministry. "Post nubila, jubila."

Crossing bayous and marshes, bottoms and bogs, sleeping out and getting lost in the pathless prairies and timbers were of frequent occurrence. But my mustang. Where is my mustang? There he is in the yard. His flowing mane, his bushy tail; his fiery look, and fierce appearance, made me proud of such a lucky acquisition. He is prancing through impatience. Two men can hardly hold him, while a third puts a wretched saddle on his back and an old rusty bit in his mouth; the bridle and reins were made of cords. My heavy saddle-bag makes him bound and stand on his hind feet. A man asked me if I were skilled in the management of horses, another if I were a good rider, and a third said that it was imprudent to ride such an unbroken horse. The men then advised me to be cautious and tie the horse, whenever I alighted; for, "if the animal once takes to the prairie or woods, you may bid him good bye," they said, "you will never see him again." The women were pitying the poor Priest. It was only then I began to realize my situation.

I am in the saddle, trembling, two men hold my mustang by the bridle. "Ready, let go."

My horse suddenly taking fright, ran away as if in a panic. I saw stars all around me. I thought that my last moment had arrived. For fully a quarter of an hour my muscular power was kept up to its utmost tension.

Thank God! my horse is calm and my fright is partly over, but for some time I trembled involuntarily with weakness.

The "Ave Maris Stella" was intoned and we went along gently for sometime, when suddenly one of the reins broke; I shivered, but bending on my mustang's mane I mended it easily. Shortly after, the same rein broke again but nearer the bit, I could not reach it. Well, I said to myself, my beast is fatigued, I shall alight and proceed to mend it. I took the lariat attached to the pommel of the saddle, and threw it to the ground so that I might easily take hold of it when I alighted. Scarcely had I put my foot on the ground when lo! O woeful moment! my mustang ran away with my saddlebag and there I was in the midst of the forest alone, twenty miles from any settlement. This happened about 3 o'clock in the afternoon. I sat on the ground and wept like a child. My poor mustang is gone, gone forever; O God, what shall I do? Ah! if I had only heeded the forebodings of those people.

I fell on my knees and said three Hail Marys adding, "O Mother dear, Immaculate Mary, give me back my horse, you see my distress." I got up, confident that Mary had heard my prayer. I proceeded a short distance, when I saw my saddlebag lying on the ground. Then a piece of the lariat, finally the saddle, all demolished. After walking about two miles, with this heavy weight on my shoulders, I became tired and threw all my equipments upon the ground except the cord. I then walked on, to see if, perchance, there were any hope left of finding my horse. I proceeded fully three miles constantly repeating the words: "O Mary, my mother, restore me my horse; O please help me to recover him." On I went, now hopeful, now sad, now confident. Lo! there was my mustang, grazing at a distance. I fell on my knees and exclaimed: "Mary, my mother, yonder is my horse, O help me to catch him." I then walked slowly, with a piece of rope in my hand and repeated at each step, "Mary help me, Mary help me." The animal did not stir, but continued grazing. I slowly approached him and placed the rope around his neck and then firmly tied it to a small tree. I trembled all over. When I recovered a little from my emotion I fell upon my knees to give thanks to God and his Blessed Mother for such visible protection. I then went back for what I had left behind. When I returned I sat down near my horse and mended my saddle and bridle.

After two hours work I was in the saddle again. About 11 o'clock p. m. I arrived at a house quite exhausted. When I recited my adventures to the landlord he offered me a gentle horse, in exchange for my mustang, but I placed my trust in Divine Providence and refused his generous offer. My mustang grew gentler and gentler every day. The next day, after having said Mass and baptized a dozen of babies and larger children, I started according to my custom for the next settlement. They told me that it was fifteen miles distant, that there was no road, and that I should be obliged to pass through the prairie to a timber nine miles distant, where I should find a path at the edge of the forest, which would lead me to a small settlement. When I arrived at the edge of the forest I discovered the path and followed it for some time. After awhile another path entering into the timber attracted my attention. I said to myself, "perhaps there are some houses over there, I shall go and see." When I advanced two or three miles into the forest, the path again forked and rendered me perplexed as to which of the two roads I should take. I called out and heard a dog barking at a distance. After a while I discovered a fence, and going around it I arrived in front of a small house, out of which came a woman, who asked me if I were a Catholic and if I knew how to christen. "Yes, madam, that is my office." "Are you a Catholic Priest?" said she. Upon declaring that I was, she cried out, "please come in quickly, there is a dying baby here." Going in I saw the baby resting on the lap of a woman. He was really dying, I immediately baptized him, then prepared my surplice and stole, opened the holy oils stock and approached the baby in order to supply the ceremonies of baptism; but he was dead.

Thanking God for my timely visit I went back to

the path at the edge of the wood and reached the settlement. There I found about fifteen grown children unbaptized, and I remained a few days to teach my catechumens. During one of my instructions there came a young man on horseback. "Are you the Priest?" he said: "My father, hearing that a Priest was around here, sent me to ask you to come quick to see a negro woman, who is dying three miles from here." I went and saw a big stout woman suffering with the colic. I administered forty drops of laudanum to her and she became well in ten minutes. The women there said it was a miracle. "Yes," said I, "it is a miracle wrought by the laudanum." The master of that woman asked me how much I wanted for my trouble. "Nothing sir," said I; he then offered me a ten dollar gold piece for my traveling expenses, as I had saved his housekeeper: a slave, whom he would not have given for four thousand dollars. I took the money as I needed it very much, since the purchase of my mustang had made a big hole in my purse. I then returned to my catechumens. A married man had just arrived from his place seven miles distant. He wished to be baptized, for he had been born of Catholic parents and wished to follow their religion. I told him that he would be obliged to come to catechism with the children. He came from his place and returned every day for five days. Then he was baptized and married, for his first marriage by the squire was null and void. A short time afterwards, the poor man was accidentally drowned while crossing a bayou. One day I met a young Creole, near a bayou, and as we were riding along together he saw a young alligator about three feet long. My companion alighted, rushed upon the ugly beast, stamped his heel upon its head and crushed it to death. Further on, we captured a beautiful turtle, weighing at least fifteen pounds, and we enjoyed a turtle soup at the next settlement.

One day on arriving at a settlement I saw a whole family in affliction. A little girl had fallen into a bayou and being caught by an alligator, had, by her piercing cries, aroused the neighbors, who seeing the ripples on the surface of the water, realized that the monster had disappeared under the water with its prey. The bayou was scoured. A large alligator was killed and ripped. In his stomach were found shreds of the poor girl's dress and her pocket knife.

Since that day, when crossing a bayou, I dreaded the ugly amphibious beast.

It may not be without interest for the reader, to note here my modes of crossing swollen creeks and bayous. At that time bridges in Calcasieu were yet among future contingents, and bayous are numerous and deep. My first method of crossing them was to hold my horse by the tail with one hand and paddle with the other. But one day seeing cow boys in the act of crossing a swoolen creek; some standing erect on their horses, others kneeling on the saddle, I tried the experiment, but my heavy saddle-bags, which, on such occasions, I generally carried tied on my head, together with my boots, prevented me from keeping my centre of gravity to the detriment of the laws of equilibrium. Experience taught me that the securest method of crossing bayous, was for me to remain in the saddle, notwithstanding the inconvenience of taking a half-bath.

After rambling over Calcasieu for nearly two months and a half I arrived at Lake Charles, where I found three Catholic families and said Mass at the house of a wealthy French lady and baptized eighteen children. To day (1899) it is a flourishing parish, with two resident Priests and an academy for young ladies. From Lake Charles I returned to Galveston via Liberty and Houston, meeting General Sam Houston on the road accompanied by a Colonel and a Major; he was stopping at a Captain's house, some twelve or fifteen miles east of Houston. On reaching Galveston I sold my mustang, which had become as mild as a lamb, to a Priest. My poor mustang, how I missed him.

Upon my arrival at Galveston I found Father Vignolle, O. M. I., supervising the construction of St. Mary's College, chatting with bricklayers on the top of the walls, which were nearly two stories high.

A frame building, which was intended for a kitchen, had been erected close to the college. The Oblate Fathers, who hitherto had lived in the Episcopal residence, occupied this modest dwelling, where they could better attend to the exigencies of community life. The society for the Propagation of the Faith had for three years allotted the Oblates a certain amount of money, to enable them to establish their mission in Texas. This subsidy was turned into bricks and mortar for the new College. But Bishop Odin having done his utmost to push the work was speaking of suspending the construction of the college and putting off its completion to better times. As the suspension of work would have been a great pity, the writer of these lines offered himself to go collecting among the rich planters of Louisiana.

Bishop Odin took up the idea favorably and wrote to Archbishop Blanc for the necessary faculties.

I started accompanied by Rev. Father Borias, who was to be installed Pastor of Beaumont. We took passage on a vessel bound for Sabine Pass. After landing we crossed the river to Johnson's Bayou to pay a visit to Captain Green, a particular friend of Bishop Odin. He made me a present of a beautiful, strong horse for my long expedition. After having spent a few days with the Captain and his excellent wife, who was a highly educated lady and a devout Catholic, we re-crossed the Sabine river. A few miles from Beaumont the Rev. Father Borias bought a horse, but before making a bargain he wished to try him. Forthwith he jumped on the beast's back from the right hand side. When the young man, the owner of the animal, saw this, he said: "Well I declare, my horse never saw that before." I left my Rev. companion at Beaumont. His whole fortune was,—$40, for I had loaned it to him, to enable him to pay for his horse.

Now let us go via Orange to my dear Calcasieu. The man whom I mentioned before as residing in a box was there, living comfortably in a fine two-story house with his wife and daughter, who had just arrived from Alsace. During dinner we chatted on the "vicissitudes of human affairs." After drinking to the health of that prosperous family, I crossed the Sabine river to visit a a few families I had not seen as yet, when to my suprise I learned that, at the time of my first visit, I had not seen one-half of Calcasieu.

In one settlement of five or six families where I staid three days I baptized fifty infants and grown children, who had been brought from a distance of fifteen or twenty miles. As soon as the people had learned from the men who had been sent all around to announce it, that the Priest was there, it was a pleasing spectacle for the missionary to see men, women, and children arriving from every direction—some in carts, others on horseback, and some again on foot. The infants were immediately baptized. The grown children were detained two or three days for instruction, previous to the reception of this sacrament. Among my catechumens was a young man twenty years old, who had never seen a Priest and who was very anxious to accompany me on my travels. A French gentleman by the name of Pujo and his wife, an American lady, rendered me invaluable services. Mr. Pujo had a "coaster" just ready to sail down the Calcasieu river. I availed myself of this God sent opportunity and baptized on both sides of the river, while the captain was selling his goods. When we arrived at the mouth of the Calcasieu river, the vessel sailed through the Gulf of Mexico to the mouth of the River Mermenteau, sixty miles distant, but I started inland, and traveled sometimes on foot and sometimes on horseback. My first day on the road I said Mass at the bedside of a dying woman, to whom I administered the last Sacraments. On the same day, it being Sunday, happening to pass by a Protestant church, I tied my horse to a fence and entered. The minister invited me to preach to his congregation. I did so, delivering a sermon on the four marks of the Church, a sermon I had already preached twelve times,—in fact, the only one I had delivered in English during my missions, repeating it whenever the occasion offered. The sermons among the Creoles were generally delivered in French.

But to compare small things with great, when Bishop Conway of Philadelphia, after having ordained the Rev. John Hughes to the Priesthood, invited him to accompany him on his pastoral visit, he advised him to have good instructions prepared for the occasion. At the first parish, Father Hughes, who afterward became the Archbishop of New York, gave his first sermon. "Well done Father Hughes, continue," said the good old Bishop. At the second place Father Hughes repeated the sermon. At the third place, came the same sermon. "You are like the cuckoo," said the Bishop, "giving the same note all the time." "Bishop," said Rev. Father Hughes, "Your Lordship told me, 'Well done, well done, continue.' If my sermon is good in one parish, is it not as good in the next, where they have not heard it as yet?" "You are right, Father Hughes, continue;" said the old Bishop.

After taking dinner with the Protestant minister I continued my mission. Two days later I arrived at the Mermenteau river, where I found the coaster waiting for me and bound for up the Mermenteau. Going up the river I baptized a number of children on both banks. Returning to Mr. Pujo's by land I started for the upper Calcasieu, where I visited a tribe of Indians called Carancawas. There I baptized eleven papooses. A Creole gentleman who spoke the dialect of the tribe, stood sponsor. The chief of the tribe, a stout man of 85 summers, who knew a little broken English, told me that a long time ago he was the owner of all the country around. His tribe, he said, was then "plenty, plenty," but now was "no more big." I baptized his daughter, aged 50. She was the servant of the French Creole, who had stood as god-father for the Indian infants. The chief's grand-daughter came from a considerable distance with her two papooses, whom I also baptized. So the chief had lived to see his great-grand-children. He said that he was the doctor of the whole district, his pharmacy consisting of the herbs, flowers, and roots of the prairie and forest of his old kingdom. Turning toward the Sabine river I met a crowd of Indians in the woods, who nearly frightened the life out of me. Were they gentle or wild? I said my act of contrition, and when they drew near I tried to look pleasant and bade them good evening. They muttered a few words and passed by. My fright abated and my heart beat more regularly. About sundown I reached a stream which I found swollen and could not cross. I got off my horse and walked up and down along the bank saying my breviary, when I heard the voices of two boys on the opposite side, who were looking for a cow. I hallooed to them, and they heard me. They told me I could cross the stream a short distance below, where a big tree had fallen across the river. My horse swam over, and I, with my saddle-bags on my back, crawled on all fours on the log as far as I could across the river; but as the last branches were too slender to rest upon, and thinking the water shallow I jumped into the stream, and found myself in five feet of water. On arriving at the nearest settlement' one mile distant, I went to bed to give my clothes an opportunity to get dry. The next morning I said Mass, baptized a few children, then started for Grand Coteau, where I arrived on Ascension Day, after four days' traveling, having been lost in the forest thirty-six hours, and having crossed fifteen swollen bayous and creeks.

The Rev. Father Roccoford, S. J., (now stationed at Washington, D. C.) looking at such a strange apparition as myself, and seeing my boots and pants covered with mud, the brim of my hat hanging over my ears, my coat full of rents, exclaimed: "Where in the name of fortune do you come from?" "From Texas via Calcasieu;" I answered. I remained with the good Jesuit Fathers eight days, for the sake of recuperating. The Rev. Father Superior made me a present of a new suit, I bought a new saddle, a new hat, and a pair of boots. Now I am ready for my begging expedition for the Galveston college; hitherto I had traveled in search of souls, now let us go for the dollars.

CHAPTER III.

An Ablegate sent by Pope Gregory XVI. A Protestant Doctor. Bayou Pierre. Shreveport. Eight Negroes Hanged. Back to Galveston. Bishop Odin, Abbe Dubuis. Father Neraz.

Always Texas and Louisiana? No, Senor. Wait a little, Mexico will come in after awhile. Mexico? Si, Senor. Then a few episodes of the civil war, and my journey from Mexico to Rome via California and New Mexico. Have patience. Deo volente, my travels episodes, incidents, and accidents of nearly half a century will be told. Traveling is a good teacher. Well did a poet understand this, when he said:

"How much a dunce that hath been sent to roam
Excels a dunce that hath been kept at home."

Now to be serious, I departed from Grand Coteau, bidding adieu to the Jesuit Fathers with a vivid recollection of services rendered to a poor missionary. My boots, hat, clothes, and saddle were brand new and the "Mendicant Friar" had a good start with bright prospects. At St. Martinville I was the guest of Rev. Father Jan, a venerable old Priest who had been sent by Pope Gregory XVI as Ablegate to the Republics of Hayti and San Domingo, to look after the condition of ecclesiastical affairs there. But as his life was at stake, he left the island and sailed for New Orleans. Archbishop Blanc offered him the rectorship of St. Martinville, which he retained until he died at the advanced age of 90. After I had seen the favorites of fortune here, I visited the rich planters of Bayou Teche, and those on the banks of the Red river up to Natchitoches, where I stayed a week with the late Very Rev. Dichary, V. G., and Rev. F. Duffo, S. J., now stationed at New Orleans.

On the road to Shreveport, I stopped at a settlement called Bayou Pierre, where I was told, that fifteen miles from the road there lived an American doctor, a Protestant, who was in the last stage of consumption and had expressed the wish of becoming a Catholic. I left "nummos pro salute animae." I found the man a mere skeleton. At the sight of the Priest, he exclaimed: "Oh, blessed be God, who has heard my prayer." After his bapsism he said: "Oh, now I shall die happy." So true it is that he who prays receives light and grace. I went back to Bayou Pierre and proceeded to Shreveport. On entering the town I inquired if there were any Catholics there. "No sir, we are all heathens here," was the answer. Later on I met a gentleman by the name of McCarthy, who was not a heathen, but a true son of Erin. He introduced me to five Catholic families. I said Mass in the court house to a large congregation the following Sunday, then baptized twenty-one children, showing that there were more than five Catholic families in the place. Mr. McCarthy gave a grand dinner in honor of the baptism of his two children, to which myself and fifteen others were invited. The people showed themselves very kind and generous to the Priest. When I had visited all the plantations on the Red river down to its mouth, I crossed the Mississippi river. About dusk I arrived at a plantation where a horrible spectacle presented itself to my eyes. Eight gibbets were erected there in the yard, where eight negroes had been hanged the day previous for having plotted against their master's life. O! what a terrible night I passed there, full of ghastly dreams.

  I left that unhallowed spot early in the morning and proceeded to Donaldsonville where I sold my horse and went on board a steamboat bound for New Orleans. Here I paid my respects to Archbishop Blanc and then started on the Gulf of Mexico for Galveston. Upon my arrival there, I found the college almost completed. In November 1854 it was opened for the reception of boarders and day-scholars.

In regard to the mission of Texas in 1855, the young Levites, who had responded to the invitation of Bishop Odin in 1852, and who had already been raised to the dignity of the Holy Priesthood, were stationed in various parts of the State. They had already tasted some of the sweets promised them by Bishop Odin, namely. "You will not always find something to eat or drink, you will be without ceasing on journeys through unknown regions where the distances are immense, the plains boundless, and the forests of vast extent. You will pass your nights on the moist earth and your days under the burning sun. You will encounter perils of every kind, you will have need of all your courage and energy." Poor Bishop Odin. He had already experienced these things himself and knew of what he was speaking. The writer of these lines remembers having heard Mr. Nash say, "The Vicar Apostolic and I lived in an old shanty and slept on a kind of shelf, similiar to a sailor's bunk. The Bishop slept in the lower berth and I in the upper."

This was in the first year of Bishop Odin's administration as Vicar Apostolic. But who was Mr. Nash? He was the faithful purveyor, book-keeper, Mass-server, and general manager of the Bishop's business for many years. The erection of a frame building, known as the Bishop's residence, greatly improved the condition of affairs. Still a Priest describing the manner of living in the Episcopal palace in a letter to a friend, said, "to give you an idea of the comfort and luxury of our life, let it suffice to say here in Galveston the whole amount of the weekly expenditure of the Vicar Apostolic and

the three Priests, who live with him, is $4. Monsignor
Odin chooses poverty and strictness and is only rich
and lavish toward the poor." In a letter which this
Apostolic Bishop, who lived upon a dollar a week, sent
to his parents, he said. "Sometimes discouragement
almost seizes me, when I know not what means to adopt
to procure even the most indispensible provisions; but
God is a good father and always comes to our help."
Abbé Dubuis wrote a letter from Castroville, which con-
cluded with these words: "To this hour I have never
known one moment of disgust or regret, and, if I were
still in France, I would quit it immediately for the missions of Texas, which I shall only abandon when
strength and life are taken from me." He and a Priest
companion were the joint proprietors of a single cassock, and as they sometimes galloped eighty miles to administer the Sacraments to a sick person, their clothes
were in a dilapidated condition; so while one said Mass,
the other was obliged to stay in the house. Even at this
hour, missionaries of the same class in Texas continue
the same valiant and patient apostolate.

One day, when traveling through Texas, (Aug 4th,
1855), I met Rev. Father Neraz all alone in the woods
100 miles from Nacogdoches, where he was residing.
Having traveled together for sometime, we camped on
the road and he prepared some coffee for me. When I
tasted it I exclaimed: "Eh! there is no sugar in your
coffee." "Sugar in my coffee," said he, "how could I
afford such a luxury, when I received only $92 during
the whole of last year." Father Neraz afterwards became Bishop of San Antonio and died in 1894. He was
certainly of genuine Episcopal timber.

CHAPTER IV.

Father Verdet, O. M. I. The ill-fated Nautilus. Nine Days Floating on a Door. Father Keralum, O. M. I. Making a Coffin. Lost in the Chapparals. Dies of Hunger. Remains found after ten years. My Fourth Tour. A Baptist Minister. Sour milk. How I Paid my Fare.

Au revoir luxuriant prairies, trees festooned with moss, landscapes varied with fields of bright green maize and with groves of dark green pines! Au revoir! From the depths of my cell I shall recall the memory of the dead! the tragic deaths of Rev. Fathers C. Verdet, P. Keralum, and P. De Lustrac, O. M. I. In the year 1856, the church at Brownsville on the Rio Grande was just emerging from its foundation. Rev. Father Verdet, Superior of the Oblate Fathers in Texas, in order to hasten the construction of the much needed church, decided to undertake a voyage to draw some funds due the mission and to purchase the lumber required for continuing the work. He embarked on the ill-fated Nautilus at Brazos Santiago and arrived at Galveston on the 9th of August at 10 a. m. At that time I was stationed at the college. How well I remember the downcast, gloomy countenance of Father Verdet as he entered my room. He had suffered from the start for two days, the steamer being tossed to and fro like a feather; the Gulf being unusually rough and the weather being stormy. It was with extreme difficulty that the boat entered the harbor at Galveston. We endeavored to induce Rev. Father Verdet to postpone his voyage and wait until the following Sunday, when it was announced that a steamer would start for New Orleans. "No," said he, "I cannot wait, I must go now." I accompanied him to the wharf. On the way we saw a gentleman kissing his family good-bye. His eyes were moistened. He had never been seen so affected. When we arrived at the wharf we heard a man saying: "that steamer will never reach New Orleans." Others said: "the wind will subside about sundown."

The Captain was advised to stay in port for a day or two, for the weather was very threatening. He answered, that he could not delay his departure, having on board 200 head of cattle. We again asked the Father not to proceed, but he said. "I must go, my fare going and returning is free. It is a God-send, our mission is so poor! To-morrow we shall reach the Mississippi."

But the next day poor Father Verdet reached eternity, and with him all the passengers and crew, except one, a negro, who remained nine days at the mercy of the waves, floating on a door. He related the catastrophe as follows:

"A violent gale struck the steamer on the starboard side, just as she was changing her course to make for land and caused her to capsize. I saw Father Verdet and the Captain, who were clinging to an overturned boat, swept into the sea by a blast of wind."

He also said that shortly before the wreck, he saw Father Verdet baptizing the Captain and his son, Edward. Poor boy! he had been prepared by me to be received into the Church and was to be baptized on his return from his vacation. How glad he was when starting to visit his mother in New Orleans. The negro had suffered terribly for the want of sleep and nourishment. He had kept himself alive by sucking sea-weed. He was rescued just in the nick of time, for then he was almost completely exhausted. It was the opinion at the time that the wreck had happened about fifteen miles from land opposite Derniere Isle, a place from which at one time 200 bathers were swept away by the sea and drowned.

Owing to this sad catastrophe, the work on the church at Brownsville had to be suspended. The Rev. Father Keralum afterwards took charge of the work, modified the original plan, and completed the building. Rev. Father Keralum, previous to his becoming a member of the society of the Oblates, had been an architect and had served in that capacity in several Departments of France. But he found himself called to a higher state of life and began his ecclesiastical studies in his 28th year, and was ordained a Priest on the 15th of February, 1852, being then 35 years old. Being a good designer and architect he was sent to Texas, to superintend the construction of the buildings to be erected in the mission entrusted to the Oblate Society. The church of the Immaculate Conception at Brownsville, will stand as a monument of his architectural ability for years to come. In fact, it is to-day the most perfect piece of Gothic architecture to be found in Texas. Father Keralum was an excellent religious and scrupulously exact in the discharge of his duties. He practised holy poverty to such an extent as to be frequently rebuked by his superiors. His delight was to wear the old cassocks, which others had cast aside. He was careful never to molest any one, and was ever ready to help his brothers in religion. Once, when he had returned from a visit to 120 ranches entrusted to his care and zeal, he reached Brownsville at 11 o'clock at night, but in order not to disturb the community, he lay down and went to sleep near the graveyard. His sight was very poor and on this account he frequently lost his way and was obliged to sleep upon the damp, cold ground. Once he lost his way and had nothing to eat for three days except mesquite beans, and the pears of the cactus plants, both growing so profusely in southwest Texas, the former is food for cattle and horses, and the latter for cattle when there is no grass or anything else for them to eat. One day a Protestant saw him walking along the street with some boards on his shoulder and a hammer in his hand. He said to his wife, who was a Catholic: "I wondered where Father Keralum was going with that strange burden. I thought to myself that he must be bound on a mission of charity. So, I followed him and saw him enter a poor jacal, or hut on the border of the town. When he arrived there, he immediately set to work to make a coffin for a poor dead woman, whose corpse was lying on the ground." Poor Father! well do I remember the last time that he went forth from our midst to visit the distant and laborious missions assigned to his loving care and apostolic zeal. Just before departing he said to me: "I have a presentment that I shall never die at home, but if I lose my way in the woods and find myself on the point of death, I shall set my horse free, for it would be a sad thing for the poor animal to die of hunger and thirst." As he set out I heard his superior say: "This is the last time I shall send him to the ranches, his sight is too bad." His presentiment turned out to be too true for he never returned.

His horse was found grazing on the prairie with its lariat hanging from its neck. The question was; what had become of the poor unfortunate missionary. Father Olivier, O. M. I., now Superior of the house at Eagle Pass, was sent out with a number of men to search for him. They searched every nook and corner between the last place which Father Keralum had visited, and the one which he intended to visit next. For several days they searched, but all in vain. No trace of him could be found. Again, what had become of him? There were many suppositions, but nothing certain.

The first, was, he had been murdered by a man, whom he had refused to marry on account of an impediment of "ligamen." The second, that he had surprised a band of rancheros, who were in the act of hanging a man, and that they killed him in order to silence the only witness of their crime. The matter remained a mystery for ten years.

A ranchero one day sent two servants after four cows that were missing. His men found the animals caught in a thicket and they could not be extricated except by cutting a way through the cacti and bushes.

The next day, they returned with the necessary tools to open a path through the thicket. After having worked for some time, one of the men exclaimed: "Eh! what is this? an old rotten saddle hanging from the limb of a tree." They came nearer and saw some human bones and a chalice. "Oh," they said, "this is certainly the place where Father Keralum died. They immediately started to inform the Justice of the Peace. Father Bretault, who was in charge of the district at that time, happened to be in the neighborhood. He was sent for. The Rev. Father, the Justice of the Peace, and several other persons, went to the spot and found a chalice, a holy oil stock, a small bell, a small holy water bottle, a piece of a rosary, eighteen dollars, eight teeth, some digital bones and a watch.

All these articles were religiously collected and taken to Brownsville. So what had been a mystery for ten years became an evident fact. The missionary had got lost, and famished and exhausted, had lain down and died.

Another Oblate, Rev. Father De Lustrac, originally a secular Priest, joined the Oblates in Brownsville in the year 1854.

In the year 1858 the yellow fever was raging in the

town and neighborhood. I was called by telegram to see a dying Irishman at Brazos Santiago, thirty-two miles from town. Father De Lustrac volunteered to go in my place. Before starting he said to me: "If I catch the yellow fever, please tell me frankly when I am in danger of death." Three days later the news came that the Father had caught the fever, after having given the last Sacraments to the sick Irishman. I rode down to Brazos Santiago and administered Extreme Unction to the sick Priest. Leaving him in the care of Mrs. Butler, an excellent Catholic lady, I returned to Brownsville. Two days later I went to see him and gave him the Holy Vaticum and said to him: "Father, you told me to speak frankly to you about your condition, if you were to catch the yellow fever. Now, I am going to speak to you frankly. You are going to die. You have only a few hours to live." "Thank God," said he." I then gave him the last absolution. Shortly after he exclaimed: "Father, let us go there, it is beautiful!" "Where?" said I. "To Heaven, of course," he replied. An hour later he was dead. Blessed are the dead who die in the Lord! His remains were interred at Point Isabel the following morning, and eleven years later they were disinterred and brought to Brownsville, where a large and sympathetic congregation came to the church to look upon his remains and those of Father Keralum, two martys of duty placed side by side on the same catafalque.

In the saddle again! Oh, how delightful it is to roam once more over prairies, through pine groves and forests, after one has passed a session as teacher in a college-class room. This year (1855) St. Mary's College received its charter by an act of the Texas Legislature and was empowered to confer University diplomas and degrees.

CHAPTER V.

San Antonio. The Mysteries of a Convent. The Girl is really Dead. What was found under the Statue. Grasshoppers. Exorcism.

Since 1855 the Galveston College has borne the grand title of St. Mary's University. During its first year's vacation it was my lot and pleasure to travel over Texas, on a half-breed American horse, with my saddle-bag, containing five hundred prospectuses of the new University. As I went along I was surprised to behold the progress which the Catholic Church was making in Texas. My starting point was Turtle Bayou, where I went to see Father Baudre, the president of the new university, who was enjoying his vacation in hunting cardinals or red birds and fishing for young alligators. On I went for Liberty, where, scarcely two years previous, I had held divine service in a private residence. There I found that a frame church had been erected and Rev. Fr. Lacour had been appointed its first resident Pastor.

At Nacogdoches Father Hagerty was teaching school, whilst Father Neraz was busy making his collection of corn, going from ranch to ranch and driving a Mexican cart. I accompanied him on one of his collecting trips. In two days he had his two-wheeled vehicle loaded with corn, which he carried home. The people could not give money for his support, so they gave him corn.

He repeated this operation until he had seen all his parishioners, giving them his blessing after receiving their "tithes of corn." II Esdras XIII. 5. Shortly after my arrival, there came from Arkansas Rev. Father Martin, and from Spann's settlement, Rev. Father Gonnard. One had come from the north about 250 miles and the other about 100 miles from the South, to settle their spiritual accounts. In those days it was strange to see five Priests gathered together in the same place, in that sparsely inhabited country. The following Monday we sang a Solemn Mass of Requiem for all the Priests, who had died in Texas. The church was crowded to witness that unwonted spectacle.

At Frelsburg, in Colorado Co., there was a church built of cheap materials, but the Pastor of that church was one of the most extraordinary men I ever saw. He was a good painter, and mechanic, and a real genius in regard to inventions. I think he had conceived the idea of the velocipede, long before the velocipede itself was ever manufactured. He could mend a watch as rapidly as the best watchmaker, and could make toys "ad infinitum." At present he is the Pastor of Fredericksburg, and although 75 years of age attends to a widely scattered parish. His name is Rev. Peter Tarrillion and he is highly esteemed by all who know him. As a man of the world he could have made a fortune, but he preferred to consecrate his life and service to the church in the wilds of Texas. I think he is the only survivor of the eighteen seminarians, who came to Texas in 1852.

I passed through Brenham, Ellinger, Independence, and LaGrange leaving a few prospectuses at each place. At LaGrange I crossed the Colorado river, and at the place where a monument had been erected to the heroes of Texas Independence I met a Baptist minister, who was just coming back from a camp-meeting. Among other droll things, he said that his church was older than the Catholic Church, for it had been founded by John the Baptist. I asked him if he could prove it, and he said that he could. I asked him how the Baptists were called, before they assumed the name of Baptists, and he said they were called Anabaptists. I then asked him what they were called before there were any Anabaptists on the face of the earth; he replied that they were called Waldeness and Albigenses. "I know the origin of these heretics, but where was your church before their appearance in the twelfth century?" "Oh," said he, "our church was hidden amongst the Lollards in England." "But before the appearance of the Lollards, where was your church?" "Well," said he, "to tell the truth, I don't know." Later on I met another minister, who assisted at my Mass, and who wanted to buy a missal, because, as he said, he knew Latin and would adapt a few passages from the Mass-book to his divine worship. One day I took breakfast with a young man, who a year previous had been a cow-boy, but who was now a licensed preacher. "Preaching," as a lady remarked, "was a better paying business for him than running after cows, and required less trouble."

Arriving at Halletsville one evening at sundown, I pushed on at a rapid pace to reach a place three miles distant, where there was a church and a Priest. When I arrived at the house the Priest could not be found. Being hungry I opened the kitchen door and found a panful of sour milk and a sack of dried apples. That, at least, was enough to keep me alive for the time being. My horse too was hungry, and for this reason I was obliged to steal a few ears of corn for him out of the Priest's cornfield, I then said my night prayers and went to bed. The next morning I put a handful of dried apples in my pocket and went in search of the Priest, who, as I was told, was at the Brushy settlement. I traveled the entire day in a zig-zag manner, till at last I saw a log-house in the forest and Father Faure with a hatchet in his hands, giving a finishing touch to the work. I asked his pardon for stealing his apples and corn. The following day, I left for Victoria where, in company with Father Anstaett, I enjoyed the hospitality of Mr. John Linn, who came to Texas early in the thirties and at that time was the only American south of the Colorado river. After having visited Goliad and its old Mission Church, which recalled to my memory Fannin's massacre, I started on my way back to Galveston, passing through prairies and forests, crossing rivers and creeks, sometimes with something and sometimes with nothing to eat; sometimes sleeping under a hospitable roof and sometimes under the broad canopy of heaven; paying my fare, when in a hotel, with old newspapers, for my purse was empty and newspapers were a great rarity in those days in the back-woods of Texas. To a certain hotel keeper, whom old newspapers would not satisfy, I gave my razor and my compass in payment. Finally, I gave a boatman my umbrella in payment for taking me from the main land to the south end of Galveston Island. I was still thirty miles from the city. Pinched by hunger I ate with gusto a well-roasted wild duck in the house of a family at the point of the island, giving in exchange for it my pocket-knife, which highly pleased the landlady.

Fifteen boarders for the University was the result of my tour through the highlands and lowlands of Texas, together with the knowledge which I acquired of things in general and the progress of the Church in particular. Still the progress of the Church was restricted to a certain limit, for, if a line were drawn from Eagle Pass through Fredericksburg and up to Nacogdoches, there would not be found a single Priest in Texas north of this line, except one at Ysleta near El Paso. If in 1855 a traveller had crossed the prairies and forests where Sherman, Denison, Fort Worth, and Dallas now stand and if he had been told that in the year 1890 there would be a diocese with a Bishop, forty Priests, eleven academies, nineteen parochial schools, and 20,000 Catholics he would have laughed at the idea and looked upon the one declaring such a thing as a dreamer. What would have been considered at that time as a dream is now an accomplished fact.

This is the end of my three years Mission through Texas and Western Louisiana. I was a happy man, in the bloom of life, with a sound constitution and a hearty appetite, having sometimes an abundance of sweet potatoes, corn-bread and bacon washed down by a certain black liquid, they called coffee; sometimes nothing but pure air and water to refresh my lungs and quiet the cravings of the inner man. Fifty times I slept under the canopy of heaven in the endless prairies and roadless forests, but happy in the consciousness of doing good.

Three hundred infants and ninety adults baptized were the principal fruit of my wanderings. These baptisms are consigned in the church records of Galveston, Beaumont: Texas; and Grand Coteau and Natchitoches: Louisiana.

Three years in the saddle! Now three years in the chair of mathematics, but with nothing worth relating beyond the daily routine of a college life. In October (1857) the Oblate Fathers of Galveston were ordered to go to Brownsville, to take part in missionary work on the frontier of Texas. Father Vignolle and I took the steamer to Indianola, and went from there to Brownsville by land. On the road our carriage was stuck in the mud a number of times, and our horse was completely worn out before we reached San Patricio. At San Patricio we purchased a strong horse to carry us through the sandy district, where we became acquainted with the tortilla. Bread in the Mexican ranches is not a wheaten loaf, but thin tortillas made from corn meal without any yeast. The women soften the corn in lime water and place it on a flat stone called a metate, and then with another stone shaped like a rolling-pin they grind the corn into a paste. This paste is then patted with the hands into thin cakes and baked quickly on a metal plate. Tortillas and frijoles (beans) are the principal food of the Mexican ranchero. This bill of fare is hardly ever changed by the poor, sometimes they have frijoles and chile (red pepper), an egg or two, chile con carne (red pepper with meat), or soft red pepper. The manner of eating tortillas and frijoles is soon learned by Americans or any others, who have been amongst the poorer class of Mexicans. They spread the beans or eggs on the thin cake, using it as a plate. Then they double up another cake, which they use as a spoon, and with this they convey the beans or eggs to the mouth. When the beans have been eaten, they consume the plate and the spoon.

We arrived at Brownsville on a Saturday. I was invited to sing Mass on the following day and to announce that, for the future, I was to be the parish Priest of the American congregation, but "Man proposes and God disposes." Just after Mass the following day Rev. Fr. Gaudet received a letter from Bishop Odin, asking him to send two Priests to San Antonio immediately, one to take charge of the Mexican congregation, which attended the church of San Fernando, and the other to take charge of the American congregation, that attended St. Mary's church. On the Monday following at 5 a. m. my companion, Rev. Father Gaye and I, were on the road to San Antonio. The journey lasted nine days; we lost one day on account of a high fever, which had attacked me. I recovered from it by drinking a bottle of wine, sweetened with quinine. Nothing of importance happened on the road, except that one day we had to cross a swollen creek by going one after the other astride a bundle of hay enclosed in a cowhide. This funny conveyance was directed across the creek by a Mexican, who was an excellent swimmer. We arrived in San Antonio on All Saints' Eve at 9 p. m. Bishop Odin invited me to sing Mass the following day in St. Mary's church at 10:30 a. m. and at the same time to announce to the congregation, that I had been appointed the parish Priest pro-tem. During the absence of Rev. Father Dubuis, who was in France. At the same time I was Chaplain of the Ursuline Convent. One day a band of tourists from the North came to San Antonio and hearing that I was the Chaplain of the Ursuline Convent, they asked me if they would be allowed to see the inside of the convent and to examine its secrets, as they had never done so before. They were all Protestants. I told them that they would be allowed with pleasure to visit the convent, examine its secrets, and converse with the nuns. I appointed the precise time when I would meet them at the convent gate and introduce them to the Sisters. At the appointed time, I found them at the convent door impatiently waiting to be admitted. They entered and were introduced to the Sisters in the community room. After talking with the nuns for some time, they were invited to visit all the apartments of the building. After doing so, they came out satisfied that there were no arms, no dark chambers, no dungeons, and no secret passage ways whatever, to be found in Catholic convents. As they left, I said to them: "You have seen one cloister, and in seeing it you have seen them all." Their conviction about the nuns was that they were very amiable and highly educated ladies.

In the month of December (1857) three gentlemen came to San Antonio from Austin. One of them was the father of a young lady who had died six months previous, while she was a boarder in the Ursuline Convent. A report was spread in Austin that the young lady was not dead, but that she had been secretly taken to another convent, or had been sent to France. The father, in order to silence this false report, had the grave and the coffin of his dead daughter opened. Two witnesses and I were present, when the white veil, which covered the face of the dead girl, was removed by her father. "Oh! poor child," said he. There were no signs of corruption as yet and her features were well preserved. An affidavit was written and signed: this silenced the false report. The young lady was a Protestant, and had several times expressed to her father her desire of becoming a Catholic. But each time her request was refused with scorn. Shortly after her death as the Sister Sacristan was cleaning and dusting in the chapel, she removed the statue of the Blessed Virgin and beneath it she found a letter written by this young lady to the Mother of God, in which she besought her to obtain for her from her Divine Son, the grace of receiving Baptism and Holy Communion. The Blessed Virgin granted the prayer, for the young lady was baptized and received her First Holy Communion three days before her happy death.

On the 20th of April (1858), the Mother Superior of the Ursuline Convent said to me in the morning after Mass: "Thank God! The grasshoppers have respected our garden so far." Clouds of these insects had spread desolation far and wide throughout the city, and myriads of these destroyers were to be seen, hopping along the ground and laying waste in a few hours all the verdure which they found in their passage. About 9 a. m. the same day, I was called to go immediately to the convent. The fell destroyers were there by the millions beginning their work of destruction on the beautiful and valuable garden. I immediately started for the scene of the dread visitation; there were thousands of these insects to the square yard. I told the Sisters to go into the chapel and say the Litany of the Saints, while I recited the Exorcisms of the Ritual. One of the Sisters, who is still alive, seeing one of these pests alighting on her sleeve, crushed it, saying at the same time, "Lord, crush them all as I do this one." After this we went to the garden and I declare that not a single one of these insects could be seen.

I am now getting old. In the year 1858 I baptized a young lady 18 years of age. I happened to meet her six weeks ago for the first time since she had been received into the Church. Seeing this venerable old lady, I said to myself, "I am getting old." Two grandsons of this lady, who is now about 58 years of age, are altar boys at St. Mary's Church. Who is the writer of these lines? this is a question asked by many. Well, I am an O. M. I., which means Oblate of Mary Immaculate, But who are the Oblates? For the benefit of those, who do not know and who are anxious to know who they are, here is a compendium of their history:

The Oblates are a society of missionary Priests, who were approved by Leo XII. This approval was given on the 17th of February A. D. 1826, and the letters of approval "in forma specifica" are dated March 21st, 1826. The congregation is at present divided into five provinces and nine Missionary Vicariates. Moreover houses have lately been established, namely, two in Holland, two in the Island of Jersey, one in Madrid in Spain, and two in Germany.

The Oblates have five missions in Texas, five in Massachusetts, and two in New York State. They have charge of half the island of Ceylon and the greater part of British North America. They have twelve establishments in England, Ireland, and Scotland, and five in Africa. The province of Canada has eleven establishments and Rome two. This ends the First Part of the Reminiscences. Part Second will treat of episodes and incidents which happened on the Mexican side of the Rio Grande, Part Third of those on the American side of the same river, and Part Fourth of my journey from Mexico to Rome.

PART II.
MEXICAN SIDE OF THE RIO GRANDE
CHAPTER I.

A Saint? The Whole Country Astir. Tatita the Impostor. A Sight. A dangerous interview. The Hypocrite tries to Arouse the Multitude. The Mayor Alarmed. Tumult. Armed Protection Necessary. Tatita Killed.

It occurred in 1860. The rumor had been current for some time that a Saint had appeared in the mountains of Nuevo Leon, Mexico, and that he was working astounding miracles, healing all kinds of diseases which man is heir to, and foretelling future events. Men, women, and children were seen on the roads leaving their homes and their occupations, in order to pay their respects to the Saint, or to be cured of some disease. Many came to consult me before undertaking the journey. My answer was "The hand of God is not shortened. What has been seen so often may be repeated for the edification of the faithful, and the conversion of sinners."

It happened at the time that Mgr. Verea, Bishop of Monterey, asked the Superior of the Missionary Oblate Fathers of Brownsville to send one of his Priests to a parish called Reynosa, situated sixty miles from Brownsville, to minister to the spiritual wants of that city which was without a Pastor. I was sent. When I arrived at the place, the Mayor of the city came to see me, saying that when it had been announced that I had arrived he and the Aldermen, who were just going to see the Saint, had resolved to go to Confession and Communion in a body before starting. The Saint had just reached a place called Mier, about sixty miles from Reynosa. I advised the Mayor and the Aldermen to postpone their journey, until I had seen the man myself. The following day was Sunday, and I said Mass, but the church was not well filled, for many of the parishioners had already gone to see the Saint. After Mass I also set out to see him, with the sole intention of investigating his claims and pretentions. Was the man a Saint or an impostor? On arriving at Camargo, which is about half way between Reynosa and Mier, I spent the night in the Priest's house, where I heard of several acts and circumstances, concerning the man, which, if true, would clearly prove that he was simply a hypocrite and an impostor. As I continued my journey I saw crowds of pilgrims on their way to visit Tatita. I also saw invalids carried to him, in vehicles of every description. I reached Mier at 8 p. m. The streets were crowded with strangers, and the principal plaza of the city was packed with human beings, all on their knees, reciting the Rosary with this singular personage, who was looked upon as a Saint. With great difficulty I approached nearer and nearer, till I came in full view of the man. He appeared to be about 60 years old, with stolid features. His hair and beard seemed unacquainted with comb and brush. He wore a kind of Franciscan garment reaching to a little below the knees, and a long cord knotted at the end, hung down by his side as far as his feet.

A Rosary with large beads hung from his neck, and he wore sandals on his feet. These were his principal external characteristics. He was kneeling before 100 lighted candles, which were stuck in the ground in the form of a cross. These candles he extinguished himself and gave as a reason for so doing, that any one else attempting to extinguish them would drop dead on the spot. Close by was a coarse, wooden cross, about five feet long, which he used to carry on his shoulders during his wanderings, which were constantly performed on foot. But here is the most curious part of the farce. He stood up and began to preach, and this is a compendium of his doctrine, which I heard distinctly: "My brethren! The new religion, which I am sent to deliver to you, was revealed to me by Almighty God Himself, for the Mexican nation. It consists exclusively in three things: To adore the Eternal Father and the Holy Cross, and to say the Rosary. Confession, Mass, and all other religious practices are abolished. Follow me, adore the Cross, and you shall be saved." This nonsense did not surprise me very much, but I was pained to see such a multitude paying the most respectful attention to his false declarations. Oh, I said to myself, for the honor of religion, this man's scheme must be frustrated. I immediately directed my steps to the Pastor of the place, who was exceedingly glad to see me. "My whole parish," he said, "has abandoned me to follow this charlatan, this diabolical hypocrite. Last Sunday I had only six women at Mass." I assured the Priest that I would do all in my power to show the people that the man, instead of being a Saint, was a dangerous impostor, teaching a heretical doctrine. When I informed the Pastor that I intended to go and see how things were going on, he exclaimed: "Don't go, for if they suspect your intention, you will not return to my house alive; I have not left my house since he arrived here. The impostor has 300 Hermanos (Brothers) armed to the teeth, who draw their share of the profits. An American is the manager of the whole affair. Be prudent, they are the dregs of society, who have found an easy way of living comfortably and pleasantly without much labor. This man, it is true, has performed some won derful cures, but all within the province of nature. His medicines are pure water, mescal, herbs and roots. He is quite successful in treating ordinary diseases, and he makes the people believe that all his cures are performed through supernatural agencies."

I understood at once, that the situation was not at all smooth; nevertheless, I resolved to act with the assistance of God, and recommending the affair to Our Blessed Mother, who always helped me in difficult circumstances, I resolved to confront the man and his followers. This man was called Tatita, which is an affectionate term for grandfather. The following day after having said Mass, I went on my self-imposed mission, thinking I should render a great service to religion, if I could succeed in exposing this huge imposture. I went directly to the place where "Father" Tatita lodged. It was a large room, situated on an elevated platform, from which a perfect view could be had of the plaza, or public square below. I passed through the crowd, and as I was doing so, I heard some of them saying: "There goes the American Priest, who is to confront Tatita." (They called me so, because all who come from the American side of the river, are called Americans.) The suspicion that I had come to investigate the whole affair and pronounce my judgment regarding it, had already entered into the minds of the crowd.

It was 10 o'clock when I ascended the platform, which was already crowded with inquisitive people. Among them I recognized two of my acquaintances, who offered to accompany me, for said they, "You may need our assistance." I entered the room where Tatita was awaiting me. He received me kindly, and brought me to an altar, in the centre of which was a large cross. He then lit two candles and invited me to say the Rosary with him. I refused to pray with him, and unceremoniously blew out the candles. I endeavored to convince the man of the evil consequences of his false doctrine, which cast odium on religion and Priests, and led the ignorant into error, but his demeanor revealed the perfect hypocrite and impostor. When he heard of my arrival, he told his Hermanos (Brothers) that the Eternal Father had revealed to him that I was forthcoming. When I told him he was doing the devil's work, feigning sanctity under the cloak of religion, deceiving the weak and the ignorant, making them believe that all his cures were the work of supernatural agencies, the better to deceive the credulous, he lifted up his eyes and exclaimed: "The Holy Cross is my protection." Then I told him that the hand of God would smite him one day, that he would die unshriven, and be dragged to hell. "Oh! but I am going to change my life," he said; "I am going to build a hermitage and lead the life of a recluse in future and do penance." Oh! the hypocrite! After lecturing the man for over an hour, I went out of his room.

The men who were at the door expressed their surprise when they saw me put out the lights and not drop dead. I spoke to the multitude from the platform. The plaza below was crowded, the Hermanos and thousands of others were there awaiting impatiently for the result of the interview. Commanding silence and attention, I said, "Brethren and Catholic Mexicans listen to me. I have left my mission for your own sakes. Keep away from this man, he is not a Saint but a hypocrite and an impostor."—Here arose a tumult of angry disapproval—But I continued:—"Our Savior said of His Apostles and Priests, 'Those who hear you, hear me, but those who despise you, despise me." Listen to my friendly voice. If this man would confine himself to administering natural remedies and not with a semblance of religion, mix heresy, superstition, and deception, with his dealings in medicines, he would be let alone. But when a man announces himself as a messenger of God, and a framer of a new religion, different from the one, holy Catholic religion, believe him not, he is a deceiver." Shortly after my friendly admonition, the two acquaintances of mine already spoken of, came to apprise me of a dangerous commotion among the crowd. They, perceiving that the cries grew louder and louder, went to consult his honor the Mayor, advising me to remain quietly on the platform until their return. After about a quarter of an hour my two friends came back, telling me that the Mayor wanted to see me in the municipal palace at once. I stepped down from the platform and accompanied by my two friends, one on each side of me and each carrying a loaded carbine, passed through the crowd and arriving at the palace we found the Mayor and the Aldermen assembled to consider the situation and save me from the perilous predicament. I was received by the Mayor with the following consoling words: "Father you are a disturber of the public peace, and according to the law I can have you arrested and put in jail. Now we are assembled to see what is the best means to pacify the people." I advised the Mayor to get 100 soldiers for protection, then by appearing before the crowd and talking kindly to them, we might be able to put down the tumult. "No," said the Mayor, "among the crowd you have desperate and unprincipled characters whom we do not know, who come from afar off and who know how to handle a stiletto, there would certainly be blood shed. Stay here, I will go myself to the plaza and study the situation." Half an hour later the Mayor came back bringing the news that Tatita had addressed the crowd, calling on them all to avenge him, and endeavor to save his mission, terribly shaken by the words of that Priest from the other side of the river. The Hermanos had sworn to take my life, and were actually preparing to come and do so. The Mayor stopped them by raising his rod of jurisdiction and telling them to desist, otherwise he would use military force, and treat them according to the law. Then the Mayor told me to leave the place at once, and that he would get fifty soldiers ready to accompany me on the road, until all danger had disappeared, "if, "said he," it had not been for my timely arrival among the crowd you would now be in eternity." The Pastor of the place seeing the turn things had taken, left the city and accompanied me, fearing for his life among those desperadoes. We arrived safely at Camargo, where we spent the night. The following day I was at Reynosa. Three days later the news came that on the day we left, if it had not been for the timely presence of the Mayor those infatuated desperadoes would have taken my life, just as I was crossing the creek that runs by the city. We also received the news that Tatita had been killed the day after my departure. Three thousand admirers of the man had left Mier. The poor man being disheartened had resolved to abandon the place, and seek for more favorable quarters. This is how the killing happened. A young man from a neighboring village gathered a certain number of comrades and resolved to go and meet Tatita on the road and kill him because he said, such a man as that would bring shame and dishonor on religion and our country. Viva Mexico! They met the man and his followers, sitting on the grass taking dinner. Tatita and one of his followers were killed, and four others wounded. Thus ended the most tragical episode of my life. Had I been consulted, my advice would have been; "Let the man go back quietly to his mountains, gather herbs, and use his knowledge for the benefit of mankind, but let him not bring discredit on religion by imposing on the innocent and the credulous the belief that he is an ambassador of God to teach a new and easy religion. God have mercy on his soul."

The parish of Reynosa had been sorely neglected for many years, and the church was in a dilapidated condition. It took me fifteen days with two men to restore the edifice to a decent appearance. The spiritual work was slower. The result of my first visit which lasted one month, was one confession heard. On a second visit I had the additional consolation of hearing two confessions. My third visit was on the occasion of the celebration of O. L. of Guadalupe; the national feast of Mexico. I first announced a grand illumination. The money poured in abundantly. In the evening the church was ablaze and two hundred lights on the tower illuminated the plaza. After the night service, the young people organized a fandango, and danced to a late hour of the night, in front of the church and I paid for the light!!! I returned to Brownsville, but not at all discouraged. During my next visit which lasted two months, sixty-five children made their first communion, and three hundred souls performed their Easter duty. This example and many others of the same nature which I witnessed during Missions given in Mexico, prove that Mexicans may be remiss, but without a doubt, their faith is built on the rock of Peter.

CHAPTER II.

Leyes de Reforma. Exiles. The Bishop of San Luis Potosi. Mgr. Verea, Bishop of Monterey. Tu quoque Ramirez!!! A Bishop Who Never Entered His Diocese. Sudden Death. Buried on Sand-Hills.

It would require a good writer to do justice to this chapter, and I do not undertake the task of relating the complete history of those times, but only a few facts which fell under my observation. The formal persecution of the Mexican Government against the clergy (both male and female) "el clero de ambos sexos" as expressed in the "laws of reform," originated in 1857. One of the first acts in the order of time was the following:

On the 30th of June, 1858, Zuazua, one of the chiefs of "La Reforma" besieged and took possession of the city of San Luis Potosi. As soon as the soldiers entered the city they ran through the streets vociferating, and ransacking the houses of those whom they thought to be opposed to their party. Some of these outlaws went to the Bishop's house and knocking at the door with the butts of their muskets, cried out, "Muera el Obispo!" (Death to the Bishop.) The Bishop came out on the balcony to confront these savages. When His Lordship appeared they grossly insulted him and one of them levelled his gun at him. The Bishop went down stairs to the court-yard "el patio," numerous shots were discharged against the door, which was finally burst open. The frantic knaves entered, headed by an officer, who cried out: "Mueran el Obispo y el clero." (Death to the Bishop and clergy.) Six days later an attorney at law, Licenciado Gomez, entered the Bishop's palace and notified His Lordship, that, by order of Zuazua, he was asked to be kind enough to give him fifty thousand dollars. "What!" said the Bishop, "Is it a dream? Miramon asked me for the loan of three thousand dollars, and I could not afford it for the simple reason, that Vidauri left me penniless by confiscating the tithes of last year, which was all that I had in my possession. The confraternities had property, but it has all been confiscated."

Then the Licenciado changed his tone of conversation, and said he was one of the best Catholics in the land;

that he knew all the precepts of the Church, but that he saw with pain that the Bishops were the cause of the revolutions in Mexico and of the bloodshed in the country, and that Zuazua would feel highly indignant at His Lordship's refusal. "I cannot help it," replied the Bishop: "for the very simple reason that I cannot give that which I have not. So, good morning, Senor Licenciado." The conference had lasted two hours before they separated. On the 14th of July, at 4 o'clock a. m., a band of soldiers headed by an officer, came to the Bishop's house bearing an order from Zuazua, condemning the Bishop and twenty-six of his Clergy to exile. "Very well," said the Bishop, "we shall be ready tomorrow."

"Not to-morrow," said the officer, "but to-day and at this very moment, and if you hesitate I have orders to shoot you dead." The ruffians did not even give the Bishop time to take his breviary. The Priests and other clerics were furnished with jaded horses or donkeys and were not even allowed time to take the most necessary articles for travel. Some had nothing on their feet but poor sandals, others were without hats, and none could get their breviaries. One of the Priests was 80 years old, another declared that he could not possibly go on horseback. "Then go on foot," said the rude and impudent officer. Thus these poor men were doomed to exile without knowing the reason why. One hundred and thirty soldiers were detailed to accompany them. It is incredible, what the Bishop and his Clergy had to suffer during their painful journey. Upon their arrival at Brownsville, the Oblate Fathers did all in their power to mitigate their sufferings and their exile.

These details are taken from a seventeen page pamphlet written by the exiled Bishop, Mgr. Peter Barajas, and printed at New Orleans in the office of the Franco-American, 136 Chartres street.

Rt. Rev. F. Verea, Bishop of Monterey, during the political troubles of Mexico in 1859-1860, came to Brownsville, and was the guest of the Oblate Fathers for nearly three months prior to his departure for Europe. His Lordship was accompanied by his secretary and two Franciscan friars, named Ramirez and Gonzales. The Bishop preached all the Lenten sermons. His homilies were very instructive and interesting, so also were his conversations, especially when relating the many episodes of his long career in the ministry as a Priest and as a Bishop. During one of his Pastoral visits, he was attacked by a band of robbers, who very respectfully demanded his money or his life. The Bishop and his secretary gave them what money they had, then the highwaymen knelt down and religiously asked the Bishop for his blessing.

After Easter the Bishop and his companions left for Rome to ask His Holiness to erect a Vicariate Apostolic in this State of Tamaulipas, then a portion of his vast diocese, a request which was granted by the Pope. Shortly after his arrival, His Lordship and his companions were given a special audience by the Holy Father, who asked the Bishop, "Have you already selected a worthy Priest to be presented for election?" "Not yet, Holy Father," replied the Bishop. Then the Pope looking at Father Ramirez asked the Bishop, "How would this man do?" "Holy Father," said the Bishop, "he is an able man, physically, mentally, and religiously." Then the Pope, addressing Father Ramirez, said, "Thou art a Bishop, go into solitude and prepare for your consecration." The newly consecrated Bishop never entered his diocese, but went to the City of Mexico, where he espoused the cause of Maximilian and became an ardent advocate of the Empire. Later on, he became the Grand Almoner of Carlota.

His Lordship was one of the four envoys chosen by the Emperor, to arrange a compromise with the Pope in regard to the "laws of reform." His Holiness could not accept the proposals of the Embassy, and emphatically declared "non possumus." Then casting an indignant look on the Bishop, he exclaimed, "Tu quoque Ramirez.!!!" The Bishop told the writer of these lines, that these words of the Pope fell upon him like a thunderbolt. The envoys then returned to the City of Mexico, where Bishop Ramirez remained until the extinction of the Empire. "Mais que diable allait-il donc faire dans cette galere!" (Moliere.) The Bishop spent some time in Havana and then came to Brownsville, where he remained eight months, being proscribed by the Republic of Mexico. His intentions were correct, but the fates were against him.

"Our wills and fates do so contrary run
That our devices still are overthrown."

On Holy Thursday, the sanctuary of our church at Brownsville presented an unwonted spectacle. Thirty tin vessels filled with oil and bearing the names of Mexico, Gaudalajara, Morelia, Puebla, Monterey, etc., were there for consecration. All the Bishops of Mexico, with the exception of the old Bishop of Durango, who was secreted and fed by an old woman, were absent from the Republic of Mexico. Bishop Ramirez consecrated the holy oils for nearly all the dioceses of the Republic. The exiled Bishop visited all our missions on the Rio Grande, administering Confirmation to people living on both sides of the river. One day His Lordship went down to the seashore for the purpose of taking a few sea baths, but unfortunately he took a bath immediately after supper, which caused his death two hours later. He was buried on the sand hills at Point Isabel. Later on his remains were removed by his successor, the Rt.

Rev. Ygnacio Montes de Oca, the present Bishop of San Luis Potosi, and placed in a more becoming locality.

CHAPTER III.

Between Two Fires. Bagdad. Oblate Fathers In Matamoros. A Hold up. Quick Justice Another Hold up. No Money For You. Stage Robbery. Remarkable Conversions.

We now enter upon a troubled period on both sides of the Rio Grande river. On the American side the whole country was in commotion; on the Mexican side, three or four parties contended for the mastery, and the Oblate Fathers were between two fires. This period lasted from 1861 to 1866. Bagdad, a mushroom city, near the mouth of the Rio Grande, in the State of Tamaulipas, Mexico, became during the Civil War in the United States a place of great importance to blockade runners, who from this point carried on a lucrative trade with Western Texas. Many families, especially from New Orleans, flocked to this place, from which during that time most of the cotton of the Southern States was exported.

During this same period Matamoras increased in population to 60,000, and Brownsville with Cameron County, to over 25,000.

Four Oblates, Fathers Olivier, Clos, Vignolle and Jaffres, were the Pastors of Matamoros and of the country around within a radius of thirty miles. At that time Brownsville, scarcely one mile distant from Matamoros, was in charge of a large community of Oblates, who, for this reason, were able to go to the assistance of their brother Priests on the Mexican side of the river when necessary. The writer of these lines was wont to visit Bagdad from time to time, in order to assist the Priests of Matamoros.

The cosmopolitan city of Bagdad was a veritable Babel, a Babylon, a whirlpool of business, pleasure and sin. A common laborer could easily gain from five to six dollars per day, while a man who owned a skiff or a lighter could make from twenty to forty dollars. The saloon and hotel keepers were reaping an abundant harvest. The gulf, for three or four miles out, was literally a forest of masts. Ten stages were running daily from Matamoros to Bagdad. One day while going to Bagdad our stage was held up by highwaymen. There were eight passengers, all Americans except myself. Upon asking the robber what he wanted, he said: "Your money!" "You shall not get one cent;" replied one of the passengers, and the driver started off at a full gallop. The robber fired three or four shots, but fortunately no one was injured. When we arrived at Bagdad, only three miles distant, we informed the commanding officer of the fact, and he at once sent a number of soldiers in pursuit of the robber. They captured him about six miles from the city. He was identified, examined, found guilty, and sentenced to be shot at 8 a. m., the following day. I spent the whole night with him; at 5 o'clock I said Mass, and at 8 a. m. he was led to the place of execution under a guard of two hundred soldiers. I asked Col. Yglesias, the commanding officer at Bagdad, to be kind enough to suspend the execution as I wished to send a telegram to General Mejia at Matamoros, asking him to grant a milder punishment, since the man appeared to be somewhat under the influence of liquor at the time of his attack on the stage. Half an hour after sending the telegram an answer came, saying "the sentence of death must be carried out immediately." I then gave him the last blessing, and at 9 a. m. he was in eternity.

Six months later as I was returning from my regular visit to Bagdad, together with seven other passengers on the American side of the river, our driver stopped the stage in order to water his mules in the historical Resaca de la Guerra, some six miles from Brownsville. Suddenly three men approached, two on one side and one on the other side of the stage, with revolvers in their hands, which they pointed at us, while one of them cried out in a stern voice: "Gentlemen, we want your money! The least resistance will be death. Take it easy, behave well, alight all from this side of the stage, fall in line, and be quick at it." I was the last in the line. Two of the robbers remained on horseback, while the third alighted and requested everyone to give up all the money which he had. One old gentleman was terribly frightened, and said with tremulous lips: "You are welcome to my money, but spare my life." "My old man," said the robber, "its your money and not your life I want." The old gentleman then gave up all his money, which amounted to about two hundred dollars, and his gold watch. The robber then went through the line and took all the money and valuables which he could find. When he came to me I said: "My dear sir, I have not a single cent for you; I am a poor Priest." "O, let him alone," said one of the robbers. The highwayman seeing the string of my cross, said: "Give me your watch." Then taking my cross from under my coat, I said to him: "That is only the cord of my cross. I do not suppose that you have a great desire for it." Then the robber on horseback repeated what he had said before, emphasizing each word. "O!—let—him—alone. Let us be off! Good-bye gentlemen, if you want your money back, come to Mexico." Then they started off at full gallop. The old man recovered from his fright, and the gentlemen who had lost their money and their watches, began making calculations. It was discovered that the robbers had obtained eight hundred dollars in money, three gold and four silver watches.

I then told them that I had one hundred and twenty dollars in my possession, part of which belonged to Mr. Anstaett, my schoolmaster at Bagdad, a nephew of Rev. Fr. Anstaett, who died at New Orleans, many years ago, and the rest to a lady for the board and tuition of her daughters in the Convent at Brownsville. "Father!" exclaimed one of the passengers, "You are smart, but you escaped being robbed by telling a lie. You told them that you had no money." My reply was, that I had no money for them, and that I had told the truth, the whole truth and nothing but the truth when I said: "I have not one cent for you." I had money, 'tis true, but it was for young Anstaett and the Convent, and not for those rascals.

When we arrived at Brownsville, we immediately informed the authorities of the adventure. A detachment of soldiers was sent out, but it was too late, for the scoundrels had reached the land of "God and Liberty."

During these troubled times, the keen-eyed business man availed himself of every circumstance to multiply his shekels. The highwayman was constantly lying in wait for a good haul, and was the terror of travelers.

Two young men, stage robbers, were in jail at Matamoros, sentenced to death. One of them had a very fine appearance and was well educated. He was the son of the governor of the State of ———. Fifty thousand dollars had been offered for his liberation, but in vain; and he was executed with his companion. On the eve of his death he joined the Catholic Church and was baptized by Rev. Father Vignolle, O. M. I.

A young American, who held a commission in the Mexican army and had become the commander of a regiment, received the grace of baptism at the hands of Rev. Father Olivier. His conversion took place under extraordinary circumstances. He had allowed himself to be bribed by the offer of a large sum of money on the part of certain American agents, and had arranged to assassinate the Mexican general at Matamoros, and to hand over the city to the Americans. A young Irish Catholic, who had refused to become a party to this wicked plot, became the means of it being frustrated, and of the culprit who had designed it, being discovered.

The misguided young officer was condemned to be shot, and was led forth to the place of execution. At that moment he flung himself at the feet of the general in command, to beg as a special favor, that a Catholic Priest might be sent for to prepare him for death. His request was granted. On the arrival of Father Olivier, the young officer earnestly requested to be baptized and to be received into the Catholic Church. "The devotedness," he exclaimed, "of the Sisters of Charity, which I witnessed in the hospitals of Louisiana, convinced me that the religion which inspired it must be true. Therefore, I wish to die a Catholic." Father Olivier obtained a delay of the execution for half an hour, in order to have time to instruct and prepare him for his death, which he met with calm fortitude and in a truly penitential spirit. Rev. Father Clos, O. M. I., now the Superior of the Mission at Roma, Tex., exercised the same ministry in behalf of another unfortunate youth, a young Spaniard, who was condemned to death, and who had resisted all the efforts of the military chaplain, that had vainly sought to induce him to prepare for death. The chaplain asked the Superior of the Oblates to appoint one of the Fathers to attend to the youth, and Father Clos was named for that sad duty. The condemned youth, in whose cell Father Clos had decided to spend the night prior to the execution, received the Priest's advances very coldly. Finally, he consented to be placed under the protection of the Blessed Virgin Mary and to wear the medal of the Immaculate Conception in her honor. In a short time a marked change came upon the youth and he flung himself at the feet of the Priest to make his confession. During the night he confessed three times, in order to prepare for Holy Communion, which he received with great fervor. Early the next morning he was led forth to execution, and his death was holy and resigned.

Bagdad has fallen! On the 5th of January, 1865, Escobedo, aided by 200 negroes from the American side, ransacked the place and obtained supplies sufficient to continue his expedition with his Lieutenant, Adolfo Garza, and a few thousand men against the Emperor Maximilian. He then started for the interior of Mexico.

CHAPTER IV.

Raid on Bagdad. A Pandemonium. St. Joseph's Protection. Bagdad is Fallen. Troubled Times. Victoria Oblate Fathers Victims of the Revolution. Civil War In Matamoros. Fall of the Maximilian.

On the 21st of December, 1865, Rev. Father A. Gaudet, Superior of the Oblates Mission in Texas and Mexico, landed at Bagdad with an accession of three new Oblate workers, to assist in the missionary labors, which had become too heavy for the shoulders of the present incumbents to bear. The population had quadrupled in two years. Father Gaudet started for Brownsville with his companions, and left at Bagdad most of the articles which he had brought from France for the missions. On the 5th of January, 1866, the startling news came that Bagdad had been raided by the combined forces of General Escobedo from the Mexican side anp 200 negroes from the American side. I was sent there in order to rescue our goods, if possible, from the rapacious raiders. When I arrived at Clarksville, a village on the Texas bank of the river, opposite Bagdad on the Mexican bank, I hired a boatman to take me over and to bring our merchandise to the Texas side, if it were not already in the hands of the robbers. At first, the boatman shrank from my request with fear, remarking, "It is hot over there." But when I offered him a generous reward, he accepted my offer. Some friends of mine, who had fled from the theatre of depredation, tried to dissuade me from crossing over, because, said they: "There is nothing but an utterly lawless gang of robbers and a pandemonium over there." In spite of their advice, we crossed the river and entered the warehouse on the opposite bank unnoticed. There were our cases of goods. We hastily put one on the skiff and set off for the Texas shore, where we safely landed it, and we had the same success with the second. But the third, containing a large statue of St Joseph, when it was already on board the skiff and was on the point of being taken over, was embargoed by an officer, who asked me what I was doing. When I told him I was simply taking what belonged to me, he said, "You are my prisoner, sir. Remain where you are until I return. I am going to receive advice from the chief;" and he went off. It was raining at the time, and I put on a rubber coat which was near by, and which by the way, I returned the next day. Since the rain was increasing and my captor did not return, I took counsel with myself and decided to escape. One! Two! Three! off we went. Through St. Joseph's protection, we reached the Texas bank safe and sound without having been exposed to any real danger. When only a few yards from the Texas shore wa were fired upon, but since the shots came in a diagonal direction, we escaped uninjured. The people of Clarksville thought that I had been shot, when they saw me fall beside the box where I sought protection, asking St. Joseph to protect me against the bullets of those desperadoes.

When we arrived at Brownsville the following day, we found that the most precious articles to the value of $200 had been taken from our cases. Bagdad was partly rebuilt, but was finally completely destroyed by a hurricane on the 8th of October, 1867, and the debris were carried by the waves into the Gulf of Mexico.

The following sketch from the pen of Rev. Robert Cooke, O. M. I., will prove interesting and show the condition and standing of the Missionary Oblates in Mexico from 1860 to 1866:

"Though the Rio Grande was the boundary line of the Oblate Missions in Texas, the expansion of the zeal of the Fathers at Brownsville was not to be confined to its northern banks.

"Mexico, that beautiful but harrassed land, extended its fertile slopes to the edge of the yellow waters of the Rio Grande. Matamoros, the first frontier town on its northeastern boundary, lay within one mile of Brownsville. Matamoros was a river port, containing at the time a floating population of from 40,000 to 60,000 inhabitants, but in its normal condition from 10,000 to 12,000, and was the commercial rival of Brownsville. The venerable parish Priest of Matamoros was not slow in appreciating the zeal and devotedness of the missionaries of Brownsville. He invited them to give missions in several parishes in Tamaulipas. At the earnest request of the Bishop of Monterey, Mgr. F. Verea, the Oblates established themselves at Victoria, the capital of the State of Tamaulipas. They also undertook the pastoral care of Matamoros and of the sanctuary and Mission of our Lady of Agualeguas in the State of Nuevo Leon."

Mexico was at that time in the throes of the revolutionary fever: nevertheless the bulk of the population remained firmly attached to the ancient faith, but helps to practice it were sadly wanted by them. Church property had been plundered by a succession of upstart governments, the good and zealous Priests were either in prison or in exile, or if allowed to remain at their posts were harrassed in the discharge of their ministry by petty interferences, cruel exactions and a continued system of threats and annoyances. Vast districts were without Priests at all and other places were, if possible, in a worse condition. Alas, their shepherds were wolves, at least on the frontier. Such was the condition of the persecuted church in Mexico at the epoch about which we write. What a field for devotedness opened up for the labors of the Oblate missionaries on their first arrival!

Victoria and its surrounding neighborhood awakened, as it were, from a long trance of faith, hope and love, in which it had lain dormant for years, under the grace of the mission given in that important town by the Oblates in 1860. After the mission a small community of Fathers was established in Victoria. During one year they labored in peace at their new missionary post, with great fruit for souls; but troubles and tribulations were in store for them. An insurrection had broken out in their neighborhood, and their expulsion was decreed by the newly installed provisional government. The inhabitants of Victoria were divided into different factions. The most numerous and best disposed part of the population manifested their deep regret at the loss they were about to sustain by the departure of the Fathers, but they were powerless to do anything more than to protest against the wrong that was being inflicted on themselves and their children by the compulsory measures used against the missionaries.

On the day fixed for the departure of the Fathers, an extraordinary assemblage filled the church to overflowing. All were clad in mourning garb to testify their deep sorrow at being deprived of the presence and services of the good Priests, whom they so much loved and venerated. Before the congregation separated after Mass had been said, a venerable lady arose and addressed all present in the following terms: "We are about to be deprived of our Priests who, because they are unwilling to prove false to their duties and betray their consciences, are to be persecuted. It may be expected that when we are deprived of the helps of religion, it will be easier to uproot from our breasts the Catholic faith—the faith of our fathers, the faith in which we were born and in which we wish to die. To-morrow the doors of this church will be closed, the house of God will be as a wilderness. From to-morrow our sick will be left to die without the Sacraments; our dead will be buried without the prayers of the Church. But are we not Christians? Should we not insist upon our rights to practice our religion, and should we not boldly demand for our Priests the liberty to exercise freely their holy ministry in our behalf?" At the close of these noble words the whole audience burst into tears. A deputation was then formed to wait upon the new Prefect, to present an energetic protest against the expulsion of the Fathers. The Prefect was alarmed by these proceedings on the part of the Catholic population of Victoria. He gave an evasive answer to the demands of the people, but all the while he was only temporizing in order to gain time to gather troops into the city, and be able thus to carry out with a strong hand, the anti-religious program of his party. Several leading Catholics were cast into prison and the Fathers were ordered to quit Victoria without further delay. A great concourse assembled to bid them adieu, and deep emotion was manifested by all present; the Fathers themselves were unable to suppress their tears.

On the 21st of December they started on their sorrowful journey. On Christmas eve they arrived at La Gavia, a large hacienda, where they were received with welcome by the inhabitants. Here they halted for some days to celebrate the holy festivals of that season, but news reaching the government at Victoria of the Fathers' presence at LaGavia, peremptory orders were despatched for their immediate departure. Their journey back to Brownsville was a very painful one, morally and physically. It occupied ten days. "We suffered much during that journey," writes Father Sivy, "the hot days were followed by very cold nights, and the rain fell in torrents at frequent intervals. While bivouacking on the open plain, we frequently had not a particle of wood or any other means to make a fire during the night. With the damp ground for our bed and a saddle for our pillow, it was not very easy to close our eyes in calm sleep."

Whilst the Fathers at Victoria were undergoing these trials, a civil war was raging at Matamoros. The inhabitants of that place refused to acknowledge the newly appointed Governor of Tamaulipas. The latter sent an army to besiege Matamoros. For three weeks the siege was carried on with great fury; over 600 men were killed, a shell struck the Fathers' house, piercing the wall, and passing exactly through the place where Father Rieux had stood one minute before. During these three terrible weeks the Fathers scarcely had any rest or sleep.

For some time after these troubles, comparative tranquillity reigned on the Mexican border. Religion began to flourish at Matamoros. Alas! these bright hopes thus aroused, were not to be realized. Father Clos writing to the Superior General says: "In my last letter I wrote to you in hopeful words, expressive of brighter prospects. I thought I was then announcing to you the end of our troubles, and the commencement of an era of quiet and of established peace. But since then, alas! revolution has followed upon revolution, and we have been living in the midst of continual tumults and anxieties. On several occasions our lives were exposed to the gravest dangers. During the last siege of the city, we were on the point of losing Father Olivier. A shell, which caused great destruction, burst quite close to him, fortunately without injuring him. At present there is a momentary lull."

Father Clos, in a letter addressed to the Superior General, dated June 28th, 1866, wrote in the following sad terms to inform him that the work of several years had been destroyed in a few days and that the labors of the Oblate Fathers in Mexico were brought abruptly to an end.

"I write to you to-day from the fulness of a heart overflowing with grief. I have sad news to give you. The mission of Matamoros is lost to us. Complete anarchy reigns in that unhappy city. The party of disorder has at last triumphed. The better portion of the population had already left the town, but we held our ground, still imagining that our work here being of a purely religious character and colorless as far as politics were concerned, we should not be interfered with; but we were grievously mistaken. On the day following the seizure of the town by the Liberals, a body of men styling themselves a commission, presented themselves at our door to ask us in the name of the newly appointed Governor, to abandon our post and to hand over to them the keys of our church. Our Superior and Parish Priest, Father Olivier, replied that we had been established at our post by the Bishop of the diocese, and that we should not willingly quit it except at his bidding, and that it was only to him or to somebody appointed by him, that we would surrender the possession of the church. On receiving this reply from Father Olivier, they immediately seized him and led him away to prison. At 2 o'clock p. m. the same day, some police agents came to our house and asked us to accompany them, under the pretext that Father Olivier wished to speak to us. When we entered the prison where he was confined, we were informed that we also were prisoners. My first thought was to ask Father Olivier whether he had had anything to eat since he had been arrested. 'I have not broken my fast to-day,' he replied. Hearing this, I at once asked the chief of the band who had arrested us, to order some food for the Father, which he refused to do.

"Alas! how little did I think when passing the night in the cell with a poor man who was to suffer death on the following day, that I with my confreres was in so short a time to be shut up in the same gloomy dungeon. He had a chair to sit on, and water to quench his thirst, but we were left to take our rest on the cold, damp floor of our fetid cell, without food or drink. Fortunately Father Parisot came from Brownsville to visit us. As an American citizen, he had influence enough to obtain an order, that we should be allowed to receive food in our prison. It seems that a cruel order to the contrary was given with the intention of starving the Fathers into submission to the impious wishes of their persecutors."

O tempora! O mores! The episode which I am about

to relate, will be read by the principal actors in the drama. Incredible as it may appear, they can testify to the truthfulness of the narration.

The star of Maximilian was waning. The United States of America had notified Napoleon III that there was no occasion and no room for a monarchy on the continent of North America. This was practically a notice for Napoleon to quit, and he fully understood it in this manner and withdrew the French troops. Maximilian was then left to his fate.

Now, the liberals were advancing triumphantly, drunk with the wine of victory. They overcame every obstacle which impeded their way to triumph. The Imperialists were completely overwhelmed, and, with their master, they received the death stroke at Queretaro, through the treason of General Lopez, the Emperor's compadre. (Maximilian had stood as sponsor at the baptism of one of Lopez' children.) Juarez is on the road from Paso del Norte, the whole country is in commotion.

As related in the previous chapter, the frontier on the Rio Grande had its episodes, one of which was the barbarous imprisonment of four Oblate Fathers. The bare brutal fact has been described. Now I shall undertake to give a full account of the savage manner in which the innocent Priests, who had been imprisoned and abused by an unprincipled soldiery, were treated. As soon as the news reached Brownsville, that Fathers Olivier and Vignolle were imprisoned, I crossed over to Matamoros in order to inquire into and investigate the reasons for such an action on the part of the new authorities. I immediately directed my steps to the Fathers' residence. When about two blocks from the house, I met Father Clos, accompanied by a constable. "Where are you going?" I asked. "I am going to jail," he answered, "and I do not know the reason why. Look out for yourself. You know how you come here, but you do not know how you are going to get out." I then proceeded on my way and entered the house, where I found Father Jaffres and a lay brother. The Father seemed to be jealous of his brother Priests, and remarked: "I do not know the reason why they spared me, for I am just as guilty as the others." After a few minutes, a policeman entered, who approached me and said: "Excuse me, Father, I have orders to arrest you and to bring you before the prefect."

"You want to make me a prisoner too, eh! Show me your warrant!" "Es por orden del Senor General Garza."—"It is by order of General Garza." I replied: "I do not belong to this parish, I have just come from Brownsville. I am an American citizen." Then seeing Father Jaffres coming out of the next room, he said: "O! that is the man I want! Sir, I have orders to arrest you; follow me." I was then left to my own reflections, walking to and fro and taking counsel with myself. After about ten minutes, I resolved to go and visit the four prisoners. On the road I met Mr. Hord, of Brownsville, who at that time was living in Matamoros near the Priest's residence. He asked me: "Are you going to jail too?" "Yes sir," said I, "but of my own accord, to see the Fathers." "Go quick," said he, "and snatch them from the grasp of those vandals, for I have heard something said which forbodes evil designs." "But, Mr. Hord, suppose they lock me in, too!" "O!, I wish they would arrest you also and put you behind the bars; I would cross over at once and bring the whole garrison to rescue you." When I arrived at the prison, I asked the Superintendent for permission to see the Fathers. "No sir, you shall not see them; they are absolutely deprived of any communication whatsoever with anyone,— son incomunicables." "By whose order? said I. "By the orders of General Garza," he replied. I started at once for the General's quarters. When I arrived there, I introduced myself and my cause, after the interchange of the conventional compliments, in the following terms:

"General I have come from Brownsville, the place where I reside, for I heard that the Priests who are in charge of the church at this place had been imprisoned. Finding this to be true, I now present myself before your Excellency, to ask you to be kind enough to inform me of the nature of the crime committed by my brother Priests, that they should be so unceremoniously cast into prison and why was the permission, which I asked to see the prisoners, so flatly refused me by the Superintendent?" His answer was: "The Priests in charge of the church at Matamoros are imprisoned by order of Senor Carvajal, Governor of the State. I merely obeyed his orders in placing the Priests in custody. The General will arrive here to-morrow morning, come and see His Excellency. With regard to a written permission to see the prisoners, my secretary will attend to it at once." A long conversation on the condition of affairs followed, in which I defined the rights of the Church, and in which also the General defined those assumed by the State. We then separated, and I turned my steps towards the jail. I first visited Father Olivier, who was shut up in a room with a guard at the door. I found the Father in a deplorable condition. He was sad, worried, and beset with anxiety at seeing his church on the point of falling into the hands of an intruder, Rev. Zertuche, whom the General had brought from Tampico and appointed Parish Priest of Matamoros by order of General Carvajal. Father Olivier had been ordered to give up his church and parish; to make an inventory of the sacred vessels and other articles, and to deliver the keys of the church to the intruder. Strict orders had been given to deprive the prisoner of food and drink, until he should submit to the demands of his captors. Father Olivier said. "They may starve me to death, or kill me, but I shall never submit to their sacrilegious schemes or betray my trust." Towards evening I ordered a lunch prepared for the prisoners, who were dinnerless. The comforting basket was soon ready, including a bottle of good wine—"Bonum vinum laetificat cor hominis." As I entered with my basket, the jailor said to me: "Were it not you, I would not let that basket pass. I only do so on account of services which you rendered me." (He had been a schoolmaster at Brownsville.) The prisoners were perfectly resigned to the will of God; remembering the words of their Divine Master: "As they have persecuted me, they will also persecute you." After a while, I returned to the Fathers' residence and packed up whatever precious articles they had and returned to Brownsville. The following day after having said Mass, I recommended the prisoners to the mercy of God and asking the especial protection of the Blessed Virgin Mary, crossed the river, hoping that the Governor had arrived with the remainder of the troops. I immediately directed my steps to the prison to inquire of the Fathers, how they had spent the night. But to my horror I was told that they could not be seen,—"son incomunicables." As I was going out I was told that they were "encapillados;" that is to say, they were placed in the dungeon where those who are sentenced to death are confined and await the day of their execution.

On the road I met Dr. McManus, a friend of ours, who told me that he had heard at a late hour of the night, that the Fathers had no beds in their dungeon and that he and his wife had provided them with comfortable bedding. At the same time I learned that the Governor, Gen. Carvajal, had arrived. I went to his quarters and asked for an audience, which was granted, but at a later hour. I insisted upon having it at once, for it was urgent. His Excellency yielded. "General," I said, "I have come from Brownsville to ask you to be kind enough to inform me what the motives are which have induced Your Excellency to imprison my brother Priests and what crime they have committed." "When we arrived near the city," said he, "I was informed that the greatest enemies to our cause were the Priests and that they have considerable influence over the people."

"You must acknowledge, General, that this is not a sufficient reason for having ordered their arrest." "My reasons are justifiable, sir, for the priests of this place are imbued with monarchical principles and on many occasions they have preached from the pulpit against our government and the cause we advocate." "I may assure Your Excellency," said I, "that the priests have been maligned and have never uttered a single word from the pulpit against your cause, and they have always contented themselves with preaching the word of God." "Again," continued the Governor, "your Priests are all Frenchmen and I wish to replace them by a Mexican Priest, whom I wish to appoint Parish Priest of Matamoros. He is favorable to our cause and is a very respectable old man and has the grade of Colonel in the Mexican army." "O General!" said I, "the fact of being a Colonel is a poor recommendation for being appointed Parish Priest; moreover, my dear sir, the Bishop alone has the power of appointing Parish Priests."

It would take too long to relate the whole conversation, which lasted over an hour. I demanded the unconditional and immediate liberation of the Fathers and I told the Governor that if I were refused, I would immediately go over to Brownsville and call upon the authorities of the American Government to deal with the case and see that the prisoners did not pass another night in custody.

The Governor asked me if I were an American citizen and upon my giving an affirmative reply, he said that it was not necessary to take such a step and that the question could be settled here, without the interference of the American Government.

"Let the priests who are in prison make an inventory of the articles belonging to the church and deliver it to me, then I shall give them their liberty."

"General," said I, "their conscience does not permit them to make the inventory which you demand, but if your excellency will be satisfied with the delivery of keys to you, I shall take upon myself the obligation of having them delivered to you."

"I accede to your proposition," said the Governor, "and I shall immediately write to General Garza, ordering him to set the Priests at liberty."

I took the letter to the General who straightway ordered the liberation of the prisoners. I then went to the church for the keys, but not for the keys of the church, as I was a stranger and had no authority to deliver them.

I took the keys of a passage-way running alongside the church: for I had not promised to deliver "the keys of the church," but simply keys in general and went to the prefect. I had to deal with shrewd foxes, and to do so, I had to show myself a gentle one. I took the keys to the prefect, together with the letter from General Garza, ordering the liberation of the prisoners. I remember that one of the officers on hearing that the prisoners were free, tore his hair and turned on his heel to show his disappointment. I then told the fathers to take the first hack they met in the street and to cross to the other side of the river at once, and that I would follow shortly.

Half an hour later, orders were given to guard all the crossings and to re-arrest the Fathers, but it was too late for they were already safe beneath the shadow of the Stars and Stripes.

Before leaving Mexico I wish to collect a few facts under one heading, in order to prove that the Mexicans in general and as a nation, are truly religious, kind-hearted, polite and hospitable. If any difficulty arises between the Church and the State, it is owing to certain laws, which, if they were examined critically before a court of equity, would be found to militate against the natural rights of a certain class of men.

Scandals are to be found, it is true, but they are to be found everywhere: "For it must needs be that scandals come." (Math. 18, 7.)

Voltaire and Co. and the great Orient are two powerful agents in the realm of Satan; still my task is not exactly to moralize and dogmatize, but to relate facts and episodes.

My first impression of Mexico dates back to A. D. 1858. The Holy Viaticum was then carried to the sick in a most ostensible and solemn manner. The church bells were chimed to announce that a Christian was preparing for the great journey from time to eternity. The Priest carried the Holy of Holies under a canopy. He was accompanied by altar boys carrying lighted tapers, and by a large number of men and women, all reciting the Rosary in a loud voice. When the sick man was in his agony, the bells were tolled, in order to call the confraternities and other pious souls into the church to implore the mercy of God on the departing Christian. O, how consoling and imposing were scenes like these! But now they are no more, for God is forbidden by law to appear in the streets. At present, processions in the streets are reserved for magnates and the celebration of certain national events. As Voltaire and the great Orient say: "Away with God!" But men pass away and God exists forever. Mexicans will die rather than abandon the inheritance left them by their ancestors.

Do you see that crowd on the plaza and in the street? They are all kneeling down on the cold pavement or in the mud, with their hats off. What is the matter? A coach is passing by and in that coach there is a Priest with two altar boys hidden behind thick curtains. The people know that Jesus is there. What a difference between 1858 and 1897; yet the faith of the people remains the same, for the true faith cannot die out in Mexico.

Once an old Priest, who was a Vicario Foraneo, and had jurisdiction over a large portion of the State of Tamaulipas, wished to have missions given in some of the distant parishes under his charge, and asked the Oblates to take charge of this Apostolic undertaking. Father Olivier and your humble servant were chosen for the work. The old Dean was the purveyor, and Remigio, his driver, executed his orders. Before starting, we placed provisions for the journey in the big ambulance, which was to convey us to our destination: they consisted of pepper, salt, coffee, bread, and a small barrel of water. When we reached our first stopping place, the Dean called out: "Remigio, go and get a kid and a dozen of eggs from that ranch yonder." The kid was obtained, killed and prepared. The fire was lit and one-half of the kid was placed on a pointed stick and broiled over the coals, and the coffee was ready. The dinner was soon despatched. At night we slept under, and the Dean in, the coach. The same program was repeated each day and night of the journey.

Do you see those twenty horsemen, wearing heavy sombreros? They were sent to meet us and to escort us to the town. As we entered, the bells chimed joyfully, and both sides of the street were crowded with people. When we came to the church the Dean went into the pulpit and after he had announced the opening of the mission, he spoke as follows: "You are expected to clean your streets, cut the weeds on the plaza, and put your houses in order, for the missionaries will visit all the families, and after this, you will see to the cleaning of your consciences." The mission lasted twenty-one days. We had never witnessed such enthusiasm, and there were very few who did not comply with the Dean's request to clean their consciences. A gentleman of considerable importance, who was looked upon as the Solomon of the place, had resolved to remain unmoved by the grace of the mission, but the grace of God gained a complete victory over him. Confession, which had appeared to him like "a pass of Thermopylae," proved to be the greatest consolation he had ever experienced. "O Father," said he, the day he received Holy Communion, "I am the happiest of men; you took a heavy weight from off my conscience. Pray for me that I may persevere!" Shortly after the mission, this reconciled Christian appeared before his merciful Creator. He was accidentally shot. "Misericordias Domini in aeternum cantabo,"

I shall now relate what happened to a man who had a yard too much of cloth on his back.

One day the Ven. Father Vignolle was sent from Brownsville to Matamoros to say Mass there, and to assist the Mexican Parish Priest, who for the time being had been left alone for the administration of the parish. The Father was seen dressed in his cassock on the porch of the church. A policeman arrested him and took him to prison. When I heard that he was in prison, I immediately crossed over to inquire about the case. The answer was that he had been caught wearing a cassock and that in order to have him set at liberty, we should pay $200. I at once tried to find the Mayor, but could not. Some one told me that he had concealed himself. As a result, the poor Father had to spend the night in prison with robbers, drunkards and desperadoes of every description. The following day the Father was summoned before the tribunal of the Mayor, where his sacred character was far from being respected. He was obliged to pay $100. Dr. McManus, of Matamoros, of whom mention has been made in these Reminiscences, stood security for him. The pious ladies were preparing to raise a collection to pay the fine, but they were prevented from doing so by the venerable ecclesiastic who had called Father Vignolle to his assistance, because he feared to incur the displeasure of the authorities. So our house at Brownsville was taxed $100 for a service rendered to a neighboring Priest.

A short time after, Rev. Father Maurel, now Superior of the mission of Brownsville, had a similar experience. He crossed the river with his cassock tucked up and well hidden under his coat. He officiated in the church at Matamoros and returned to the river. While stepping into the ferry boat, he let down his cassock and said; "I am all right, now." As soon as he had done so, a policeman approached the boat and ordered Father Maurel to come out and to accompany him to the police station and from there to the jail. There he remained till 10 p. m., when he offered $25 instead of $200, the regular fine, which was accepted. He was liberated and gladly returned to the land of the free.

On the 23rd of March, 1875, there came the last batch of twenty two Sisters of Charity. The Sister Superior was Mother Lacour. They were accompanied by Father Frias, Lazarist, of Mexico, and the Rev. Fr. Planchet, a French Priest of Monterey. They arrived by the steamer from Rio Grande City and remained the night on the boat. The next day the clergy of Brownsville went out to meet them and accompany them to the church in procession. While on their way the church bells pealed a joyous welcome. The Rt. Rev. Bishop Manucy celebrated Mass, during which ceremony the church was crowded with citizens. At the end of Mass the Bishop delivered a very touching discourse. The Sisters were then conducted to the convent where breakfast had been prepared for them. Our Sisters of the Incarnate Word gave up their beds, they themselves retiring to the upper story, which they tenanted for a whole week. The closing account will be given in Part III, where I speak of the affairs happening on the Texas side of the Rio Grande.

PART III.
ON THE TEXAS SIDE OF THE RIO GRANDE.

CHAPTER I.

Bishop Odin. Difficulties about the Boundary Line. His Honor the Mayor. A Crust of Bread. Physical Aspect. Religious Ditto. Field of Labor. First House of Worship. First Residence.

In opening this chapter, I dedicate a few words to the memory of the heroic pioneer Bishop of Texas, Jean Marie Odin, a name revered by all, a name to be ever associated with the recital of heroic deeds of humility, charity, faith, and zeal for the glory of God.

If the true conditions of zeal are, that it be prudent, disinterested and intrepid, they were all exemplified in this saintly Bishop. In this short sketch, I shall merely narrate a few facts which I have never seen in print. They will reveal the great self-denial and sincere humility of Bishop Odin.

How well I remember his return in 1853 from a visit to some of the remote parts of his extensive diocese! He was poorer than St. Francis of Assisium, and looked more like St. Benedict Labre than a Bishop. His coat was torn and faded, and his hat and shoes were in a wretched condition.

In the Summer of 1854, he set out upon a visitation of some missions, which was to occupy four months. During this journey he traversed the valley of the Rio Grande, where he confirmed 1,123 persons. While making this visitation Bishop Odin formed the agreeable acquaintance of Bishop Verea, who at the same time was visiting missions on the opposite side of the Rio Grande. The two prelates met at a ranch called Las Tortillas, where they considered the vexed question of the boundary of the two countries with regard to the celebration of marriages. Before examining the right of jurisdiction it is necessary to explain the civil side of the question. According to the Treaty of Guadalupe, the boundary line between the two countries is the middle of the river, that is to say, where the middle of the river was at the time of the treaty. It frequently happens that during a flood, the river changes its bed in many places. Sometimes the torrent steals from Mexico, and sometimes from Texas, tracts of land fifty and 100 acres in extent. According to the treaty, that which is taken from the Mexican territory remains subject to Mexican legislation although it has been placed on the Texas side of the river, and that which is taken from Texas territory remains subject to the laws of Texas, although it has been placed on the Mexican side of the river. These tracts of land thrown on either side of the river are called bancos. Now, the question was, could a Priest, having jurisdiction on the Texas side of the river, marry a couple living on a banco on the Mexican side of this river, when the banco is considered by the treaty, Texan territory? And, again, could the same Priest perform this ceremony on a banco on the Texas side of the river, although it was considered Mexican territory, according to the same treaty?

After having settled this and other questions, the two Bishops separated. Shortly after this amicable meeting; Bishop Odin was invited by the Parish Priest and the Mayor to visit the city of Reynosa, on the Mexican side of the river. The Bishop, who was at the time on the American side of the river at some distance from Reynosa, accepted the invitation. In the meantime, the

Mayor requested the best houses to be in readiness to receive the Bishop and his retinue. Places were carefully prepared for the attendants and stables were provided for the horses and mules. On the day appointed for the Bishop's arrival, His Honor, the Mayor, and the Aldermen assembled early in the morning at the municipal palace, and the horsemen on the plaza, ready to go and meet the Bishop. Suddenly a voice was heard, "the Bishop is coming!" Looking in the direction indicated, a man was seen driving in an old buggy. "No," said they, "that cannot be the Bishop." A few minutes later, His Lordship alighted on the plaza, without a single attendant, having arrived sooner than he had been expected. All this was related to me by Juan Chapa, the Mayor of the place at that time. "I never saw," said he, "such an humble and amiable Bishop."

On his second visit to the lower Rio Grande, which was in the month of September, 1858, I accompanied Bishop Odin to Point Isabel, the seaport of Cameron county, where he confirmed a good number of children. The following day we started back for Brownsville, a distance of thirty miles, by an old road and a muddy one at that. It took us the whole day to return. During the journey, he saw a piece of bread in my grip and asked me if I could part with it, for he was very hungry. "Bishop," I said, "You are welcome to it, but I fear that you will break your teeth if you try to eat it. That piece of bread has been fifteen days in my grip, that is, since my last trip." The Bishop made the sign of the cross and ate the hard bread with relish, remarking that during his first trips through Texas, he always kept a piece of corn bread in his saddle-bag, in case he might be unable to reach a house before night. "How many times," said he, "have I slept out on the vast prairies, or in the forests of Texas, spreading my blanket on the ground and using my saddle as a pillow. In cases like these," said he, "I always found a piece of corn bread to be a delicious supper, seasoned with a good appetite." During this same trip, the Bishop told me that on one occasion he waded for six miles over a prairie covered with two or three feet of water, with his saddlebag on his shoulders and leading his horse by the lariat. I do not remember the reason why he went on foot and not on horseback through the water, but I remember he told me that he sat down exhausted when he reached dry land. The reason why the Bishop went on foot might very probably be explained by the following accident which happened to me in 1854 in Calcasieu, while crossing a large sheet of water, when my horse and myself, fell into a hole, at least six feet deep. On reaching the opposite bank, I found that my vestments and altar linen had been all soaked. To avoid a similar accident, was, I suppose, the reason why the Bishop waded through the water, with his saddle-bag on his shoulders. During that journey he visited the whole south-western portion of his diocese, traveling nearly 2,000 miles and confirming 3,413 persons.

On another occasion, he told me that when he had been knocked overboard by a shifting boom in sight of Indianola, and remained twenty minutes in the water, he was saved from drowning—for he could not swim,—by the special protection of Mary Immaculate, whom he invoked in his danger.

The Very Rev. Father Chambodut, V. G., relates that when Bishop Odin left his residence in Galveston to take possession of the Archiepiscopal see of New Orleans, he refused to be accompanied to the wharf and went alone, he himself carrying his valise. Every act of this saintly Bishop exemplifies his Christian simplicity and profound humility.

It is generally admitted that the boy is father to the man, and young Odin inherited devotion to the Blessed Virgin Mary from his pious parents. During his entire life this venerable servant of God was remarkable for his devotion to the Blessed Virgin; his love for recollected and devotional life, and his great zeal for the religious advancement of others. His simplicity, ability and gentleness gained him a host of friends. By his missionary labors he accomplished a vast amount of good, which places him amongst the most distinguished missionaries of our country.

Before relating the many episodes and strange incidents which occured on the Rio Grande, we invite our readers to accompany us to the south-western limits of that territory where the Rio Grande flows under skies of cloudless blue, and empties itself into the Gulf of Mexico. Texas has received the title of "Italy of the West," by reason of its resemblance in sky and landscape to the most beautiful and favored of European lands. Surely one would think that amidst such cheering accessories of climate and scenery, missionary labor would become a bright and pleasant duty. But the trials of the Missionary Fathers will be shown to come more from men than from things. The chief promoters of their griefs will not be the unbaptized, but men who have sinned against the Holy Ghost by rejecting their ancestral faith. The following description of men and things we take from the annals of the congregation of Oblates, in the "Life of Monsignor de Mazenod, and the labors of the Oblates of Mary," by the Rev. Robert Cooke, O. M. I.

"The unhappy frontiers of Texas were the battle ground over which rolled the full tide of war with all its concomitant evils. Brownsville rose from a soil still reeking with the horrors of the battle plain. It received its name from a victorious captain in the American army.

Its population at the time our story begins was of a strange and motley character. Divers nations of Europe, the American States, and the cities, towns and hamlets of Mexico were represented at Brownsville, and not as a rule by the wisest and best of their respective populations. Hither many came, it is true, with motives that were praiseworthy, and with the laudable purpose of promoting the proper interests of life, but multitudes also flocked hither as refugees from the pursuit of justice or as adventurers who were as willing to promote earthly fortunes by foul means, as by those that were fair and honorable. Public authority could scarcely be said to exist at that time in Texas. Within a decade of years almost as many different forms of government had sprung up in succession, no time being given for any system of public law to become established, or to acquire the prestige necessary to gain authority. The law of might prevailed widely over that of right. Great crimes committed in open day, remained unpunished and men depended for protection more upon their own witty brains and stout arms, than upon the shelter of the laws of the country. This chaotic state of society was an obstacle not only to moral, but also to material progress. The situation of Brownsville, standing on a noble river that placed it in easy communication with the towns and cities of Northern Mexico ready to become purchasers in its marts, with tracts of some of the most fertile lands in the world stretching out in its rear to the north and to the east in a wilderness of beauty and productiveness, until hundreds of miles of landscape, rich in every variety of fruit and flower, met the rolling prairie or luxuriant forest—the situation, we say, of Brownsville, should already have secured for it, brief though the days of its existence were, a place amongst the foremost of the rising young cities of the West. But a moral blight was on the place, which marred its progress—the blight of irreligion.

"To remove this blight, the public mind, though deeply tinged with infidelity, bethought itself instinctively of an efficacious remedy,—the restoration of the Catholic religion and worship, which had been suspended in Brownsville since the expulsion of the Mexicans. In view of securing this object the heads of the town put themselves in communication with the Bishop of Galveston. His Lordship was overjoyed at their proposal, giving them credit for sentiments of which, unfortunately, they were not possessed. He thought it was a religious motive that had induced them to apply to him for Priests and for the restoration of Catholic worship in Brownsville; whereas their object in making such an application was of a purely secular character. They wished by the introduction of Catholic missionaries into Brownsville, to induce Mexican and American Catholics of position and respectability to establish themselves in that city, and thus contribute to its mercantile and social importance.

"Early in December, 1849, the first Oblate Missionaries, Fathers Telmon, and Soulerin arrived in Brownsville at the invitation of the Bishop of Galveston, to take charge of a district which extended in length from the Gulf of Mexico over 200 miles running west along the northern bank of the Rio Grande. In width, it stretched out in a north-easterly direction about 100 miles toward the interior of the country. We would here anticipate what will become visible as our narrative of the Oblate Mission advances, by acknowledging at once that we have no widespread and extraordinary results of missionary effort to speak of,—no fruits of zeal, commensurate with the devotedness, the self-sacrifice, the piety, and the learning of the Fathers engaged in that difficult field of apostolic labor, to describe.

"The most crucial test of apostolic zeal is that of devoted labour for souls not followed by any visible fruit. To this test have the labours of apostolic men in divers ages of the Church been subjected. Many devoted missionary spirits, from the days of the Apostles down to our own times, have had no other post assigned to them by the Divine Master in the vineyard of zeal, during their life's day, than that of being sowers only of the seed. Their appointed occupation was to plough, to harrow, and to plant, but seldom or never to reap. The seed planted by them may take a score, or fifty, or a hundred years to ripen, but it ripens in the end. They were often perhaps, in their day, twitted because no visible success followed their labors, whilst in their own hearts they had to do battle against a growing despondency; but being of the true Apostolic type, they still worked on undaunted for God and souls though seemingly unsuccessful. Going, they went and wept, casting the seed, watering the ground on which they labored with their tears, and often with their hearts' blood.

"It was laboring thus without much visible fruit that, during the early ages of the Church, band after band of martyr Apostles followed one another in the blessed winter drudgery of Christ's vineyard under blast and chill and drenching skies, and reproach and taunt and violent opposition of wicked men who hated the Word, whose seed these holy workers were engaged in planting. The sowers had done their appointed work and they were called home at eventide to receive their hire. The winter passes away, the harvest ripens everywhere, Jerusalem begins to bud forth and blossom, the voice of the turtle dove is heard in the land, the desert rejoices and flourishes like the lily, the fig tree puts forth its green figs, the vine flower yields its sweet smell. 'Arise, arise, put on thy strength, O Sion! put on the garments of thy glory. O City of the Holy One! loose the bonds from off thy neck. O Church of Jesus Christ! come forth from the catacombs, the harvest is ripe upon the plains, send forth thy reapers in great numbers. The nations are coming to thee with their gifts, the kings of the earth are to be thy foster-fathers.' Oh, blessed the hands that have sowed the seed that has grown up into such glorious harvest fruits, the conversion of nations; and blessed are they who at this hour are willingly, because God wills it, engaged in some solitary missionary work, uncheered by comfort from without, who work zealously, although without much result that is apparent, in the field of some uninviting missionary duty. Such work is highly supernatural, is productive of loftiest merit, resembles very much the work of some of the greatest Saints; yea, it resembles that of Jesus in Nazareth. Unfruitful it may seem for the while, but by and by in God's time the blossoming and the ripening will take place, and other hands, if not one's own, will garner the fruits of the goodly tree planted with such difficulty, and cared for with such loving, patient, industry, during the long winter tide."

Such reflections are forced upon us as we consider the disappointments and mishaps, the trials and persecutions, and limited success of the first years of the missionary labors of the Oblates of Mary in Texas.

The news of the arrival of the missionary Fathers in Brownsville circulated rapidly through the town. A meeting of some of the principal inhabitants took place, to which the fathers were invited, on the evening of the day of their arrival. The meeting, which was held in an empty wooden structure was composed almost exclusively of non-Catholics,—Jews, Mormons, professed Infidels, and Protestants of different sects. An aged speaker, one of the leading inhabitants, arose to bid welcome to the

Fathers in the name of his townsmen. In doing so, he made it clearly understood that the object those present had in view, in making such a demonstration to welcome the Fathers to Brownsville, had nothing of a religious character about it. Before the meeting separated, a discussion ensued as to the measures to be adopted for providing a residence and means of support for the Fathers. The first resolution adopted by the meeting on this subject was not one that gave augury of much generosity towards the Fathers on the part of the inhabitants of Brownsville. The lodging assigned to them by the meeting was the half-ruined shed, in which they were then assembled. This consisted of one apartment, unfurnished, without a fire-place, the dimensions of which were twenty-five feet by twelve. It had been a small cotton store; the floor was saturated with filth, the place infested with rats, and with huge spiders whose webs covered the walls and ceiling. Such was the first community residence of the Oblates of Mary in Texas. It was furthur agreed at the meeting that a monthly collection should be made in the town for their support.

The feast of the Immaculate Conception was approaching, and some place must be provided where Mass could be said publicly on that great solemnity. With some difficulty an empty shop was secured, the counter of which became the first altar on which the Holy Sacrifice of the Mass was publicly celebrated by the Oblates of Mary in Brownsville. The humble temporary altar was fitted up with as much beauty of decoration as their ability and the small means at their disposal enabled them to impart to it. The attendance at the services was very sparse at the outset; some slight improvement however, began to make itself manifest, when the rising hopes of the missionaries received a rude check by the "notice to quit" which reached them from the owner of their temporary chapel. For some weeks they and their little flock, were left without a place of public worship. At last a German Lutheran, whose wife was a Catholic, allowed them to have the use, for a time, of a small empty shop, which was at his disposal. In the meantime, a piece of ground was purchased and a temporary wooden chapel erected upon it.

The numbers attending services began sensibly to increase and several signs of brighter promise became visible. On the other hand, the public subscriptions which had been promised for their support ceased, and a series of other difficulties presented themselves in succession; worry and anxiety began painfully to tell on the health of the Fathers. Under these circumstances, after much hesitation, Monsignor de Mazenod came to the decision of withdrawing his missionaries altogether from Texas, to the great regret of Monsignor Odin, the Bishop of Galveston. One year after the departure of the Fathers from Brownsville, the Bishop of Galveston visited Europe. One of the principal objects of his journey was to place before Monsignor de Mazenod the great spiritual privations to which a large portion of his flock were subjected, owing to the withdrawal of the Oblate missionaries from his diocese.

He pleaded his cause so well that the great missionary heart of Mgr. de Mazenod was moved to reconsider the decision relative to the mission of Texas, and forthwith to send to that country six Fathers and a lay brother. After an interval of one year and six months absence, the Oblate missionaries, including Father Gaudet, their Superior, resumed their work at Brownsville, where they arrived in the beginning of October, 1852. Three years later they laid the foundation of a large and permanent church, to replace the temporary wooden structure which they were then using. This building was completed in 1859, and was solemnly blessed by Mgr. Odin, on the feast of Pentecost in that year. It was then acknowledged to be the finest public building in Texas. Attached to the church was a suitable community house for the Fathers.

Educational works of considerable importance were set on foot by the Fathers of Brownsville. A teaching community, the Sisters of the Incarnate Word, was established there. Boys' schools were also opened.

The missionaries had now the consolation of seeing crowds flocking to the services of their new and beautiful church. The attendance at public Mass on Sundays in the early days of their temporary church sometimes used to sink down to five or six persons, and on one occasion there was only one person present; now the church is crowded at several Masses. This awakening of faith greatly rejoiced the hearts of the missionaries. Their labors, however, were not confined to the population of Brownsville. Their vast district extending along the banks of the Rio Grande in one direction, and in the other, stretching far away into the interior of Texas, was interspersed with numerous ranches, which had to be visited at appointed intervals. Besides these, there was a large number of detached habitations scattered over the wide plains and prairies or buried in great forests, which they had also to visit. The labor imposed on the Fathers in visiting the inhabitants of these plains and forests of their district was enormous. It is true they performed their journeys for the most part on horseback; nevertheless they had great fatigue to endure and sometimes great dangers to encounter, especially in fording swollen and rapid rivers. When a missionary arrives, after a long day's ride under a broiling sun at the ranch to which he has been journeying, great discomforts as a rule await him. The huts composing the ranch are very miserable structures. A few poles are fixed in the ground; these are interlaced with branches of trees, and the whole interior is then coated with mud. Such is the habitation which is offered the missionary on his arrival by some poor family, who are glad to give him a corner in their hut and share their unsavory tortilla cake with him. He spreads his blanket upon the mud floor of his humble abode, and using his saddle for a pillow, tries to sleep, but often he fails in the attempt, notwithstanding his fatigue. The stench and filth of the place, the biting of mosquitoes, and the attacks of other insects of a more hateful type prevent him frequently from enjoying the rest he so much needs. The inhabitants of these ranches are of Mexican origin. They are full of reverence for the Priest, but, owing to their isolation and the difficulty of giving them religious instruction, they are often found to be very ignorant, especially in remote places that can be but seldom visited by the Fathers. During his stay in their midst the Father gives instructions and hears Confessions; baptizes; marries; corrects abuses, and adjudicates quarrels. He leaves one ranch to pursue his Apostolic labors in the next, and so on until he has completed his circuit of visits.

CHAPTER II.

From the Archives of the Vatican and Copenhagen. Interesting notes on America Mexico and Texas. Correspondence between d'Alarconne and De la Harpe.

In this chapter I shall follow the Codex Historicus of the Mission of Brownsville, selecting the events which may prove interesting to the readers.

Some historical data which I found on a sheet of paper added afterwards to the codex, may be prefixed before I enter into the body of my narration.

The archives of the Vatican and those of Copenhagen reveal the following facts:

1. In 829 America was visited by Catholic missionaries.

2. In 834 Pope Gregory IV granted to Ansgar, Archbishop of Hamburg, jurisdiction over Iceland and Greenland.

3. In 1004 those countries were Catholic, and it is a well asserted fact that in 1055, Adalbert, Archbishop of Bremen, Hamburg, consecrated as his suffragan, John, Bishop of Skolhold, and sent him to Iceland. He also consecrated Albert as Bishop of Gardar, and sent him to Greenland.

4. In 1059 Bishop John of Skohold, a Scotchman by birth, went to visit a colony of Icelanders, Norwegians, Danes, and Swedes, established in Vineland, and preached also to the natives of that country, co-extensive with the present New England States.

5. This same Bishop of Skolhold became a martyr, having been killed by the natives. A Priest by the name of Thornwald, was also killed by the Esquimos near the place now occupied by the city of Boston.

6. The first baptism was administered in 1009 in the State of Rhode Island. The person's name was Snowe, and the parents were Torfina and Gudrida. They went back to Iceland, and Gudrida, having become a widow, went to Rome, where, under her direction, maps of these new countries were drawn. Gudrida returned to Iceland, where she became a nun. Three of her sons became Bishops in Iceland. The last of her decendants was Magnus Stephenson, who died in 1833.

7. In 1121 Bishop Erick of Gardar visited Vineland where he died. It is believed that the monument dis-

covered near Newport dates from the time of Erick. It is a baptismal font or baptistery of the same make as those found in Greenland at Igalikho, Kakortok, and Iglorsoit.

8. The Bishops of Iceland and Greenland, suffragans of Hamburg since 834, became suffragans of Lund in 1099 by a Bull of Urban II, and subsequently became suffragans of Drontheim in Norway by a Bull issued by Pope Anastasius IV in 1154.

9. The Popes John XXI, Nicholas III, and Martin V, speak of those churches as being flourishing.

10. In 1540 Christian, King of Denmark, sent Lutheran preachers who poisoned Augmond, Bishop of Skolhold, and beheaded Arleson, Bishop of Horleim. The last Bishop of Gardar was Vincent, who was consecrated in 1537.

11. A monument was discovered, fifteen miles from Washington, which attests the antiquity of the American Church; it is a tombstone bearing a Christian inscription with the date 1051.

NOTES ON MEXICO.

1. Prehistoric ruins, ancient cities and temples unearthed, reared by primitive races, are seen in many places.

2. The character of the monuments of the ancient inhabitants of Mexico reminds us of the primitive civilization of Egypt.

3. The hieroglyphics, images, pyramids, temples add to the indecision whether Mexico is older than Egypt or Egypt older than Mexico.

4. Palenque, Uxmal and other ruins in Oaxaca and Yucatan reveal a civilization anterior to the Toltecs.

5. The national traditions have preserved the mem-

ory of an immense invasion of the Mexican territory by the Toltecs in the 7th century.

6. Some Franciscan Friars, after inspecting the crosses, images, altars, and temples at Palenque, are of the opinion that the inhabitants of Palenque and the surrounding country were Christians, and that probably their existence there dates back to the 3rd century.

7. After the Toltecs came other tribes. The most notable are the Chichimecas, from whom came the eleven Kings who ruled over Mexico until the arrival of the Aztecs.

8. The Aztecs founded the City of Mexico in 1325.

9. The Aztecs, after an aristocratic reign of short duration, elected a King in 1352.

10. Montezuma and his successors from 1436 to 1482 extended their conquests to the farthest limits of the country.

11. Montezuma II received Cortez on the 8th of November, 1519, and was subsequently killed.

12. Guatemozin is made prisoner. The City of Mexico surrenders on the 15th of August, 1527.

13. Guatemozin put to death by order of Cortez.

NOTES ON TEXAS.

1. The first European settlement, within the limits of what is now the State of Texas, was planted by La Salle in February, 1685.

2. Previous to this, the country had been occupied only by scattered Indian tribes.

4. La Salle, entering the Espiritu Santo Bay, built a fort on the spot subsequently occupied by the Bahia mission.

4. In the fort he left about twenty persons under Barbier with Fathers Membre and Leclerq, and the Sulpitian Fathers, Rev. Chefdeville, Cavalier, and Doucey.

5. For two years these five Priests offered the Holy Sacrifice and administered the Sacraments.

6. The Spaniards in Mexico, hearing that the French had constructed a fort in Texas, sent Alonzo de Leon in 1689, with a small force against the French colony, but they found it destroyed by the Indians.

7. In 1691 Don Domingo Teran, Governor of Coahuila and Texas, planted several settlements in Texas in order to assert the claims of the Spaniards to the land.

8. The Spaniards established the Presidio of San Francisco Solano, San Ildefonso and San Jose on the left side of the Rio Grande, which in 1718 were transferred to San Antonio de Valero, the present city of San Antonio.

9. The French at Natchitoches led by La Harpe and St. Denis advance westward as far as Nacogdoches.

10. The Spanish Viceroy in Mexico appoints Don Martin D'Alarconne Governor of Texas.

11. Young Hucherau de St. Denis proceeds from Nacogdoches westward across the country to the Rio Grande, on a tour of inspection.

12. All these manœuvres arouse antagonism on both sides. The French are wroth to see the Spaniards encroaching on Texas from the West, and the Spaniards are incensed at the French occupying Texas on the East. Hence comes the following spicy correspondence:

13. D'ALARCONNE TO MONSIEUR LA HARPE.

"Monsieur: The orders I have received from the King, my master, are to maintain a good understanding with the French of Louisiana; my own inclinations lead me equally to afford them all the services that depend upon me. But I am compelled to say that your arrival at the Nassonite village surprises me much. Your Governor could not be ignorant of the fact that the post you occupy belongs to my government, and all the lands west of the Nassonites depend upon New Mexico. I counsel you to inform Mr. Bienville of this, or you will force me to oblige you to abandon lands that the French have no right to occupy. I have the honor, &c.;

D. A'LARCONNE.

Trinity River, May 20th, 1719."

14. REPLY OF LA HARPE.

"Monsieur: The order from his Catholic Majesty to maintain a good understanding with the French of Louisiana, and the kind intentions you have yourself expressed toward them, accord but little with your proceedings. Permit me to apprise you that Mr. de Bienville is perfectly informed of the limits of his government, and is very certain that the post of Nassonite does not depend upon the dominions of his Catholic Majesty. He knows also that the Province of Las Tekas (Las Tekas, Las Tejas, Texas), of which you say you are Governor, is a part of Louisiana. Mr. De La Salle took possession in 1685 in the name of his most Christian Majesty, and since then the above possession has been renewed from time to time.

Respecting the post of Nassonite, I cannot comprehend by what right you pretend that it forms part of New Mexico. I beg leave to represent to you that Don Antonio de Minoir, who discovered New Mexico in 1683, never penetrated east of that Province or the Rio Bravo. It was the French who first made alliances with the savage tribes in this region, and it is natural to conclude that a river that flows into the Mississippi and the lands it waters belong to the King, my master. If you do me the pleasure to come into this quarter, I will convince you that I hold a post I know how to defend. I have the honor, &c.,

DE LA HARPE.

Nassonite, July 8th, 1719."

CHAPTER III.

Cortina. Raid on Brownsville. Impromptu Army. Took to Their Heels. Captain W. G. Tobin. Col. Rip Ford. Cortina Defeated. Three Men Hanged. Looked upon as a Spy. A Lawyer Without a License.

In the month of September, 1859, J. N. Cortina, a ranchero whose residence was situated on the left bank of the Rio Grande, about nine miles distant from Brownsville, came down at the head of fifty men and took possession of the city shortly after midnight. His object was the assassination of twelve citizens. For some time past his mind had been brooding revenge on several Americans who, he supposed, had taken unjust possession of lands belonging to his countrymen, and who, he imagined, were unfriendly to the Mexican race. For three or four hours he occupied the city, during which time he killed six Americans. Organized resistance was out of the question. The Americans, terror-stricken, had only time to look for hiding places. At day-break the assassin and his accomplices withdrew to his ranch. There he did not remain inactive. His little army of fifty increased daily and soon numbered as many as 200 well-armed men. The prospect was gloomy. Many inhabitants had crossed the river to Matamoros to find a place of security. The enemy had erected fortifications or earth-works at a sharp turn of the road, about one mile above Cortina's ranch.

The Brownsvillians, fearing a second attack, barricaded the central portion of the city with two cannons for defense.

One day, stirred up by a bellicose frenzy, they resolved to enlist all the men capable of bearing arms, both old and young, then to go and rout the enemy; force them to bite the dust or cross the river.

Two hundred men volunteered to go and meet the enemy. A General was elected to command the expedition. There were Captains; Lieutenants; Sergeants and privates. The regular army of Fort Brown had been reduced to only a few men, most of the soldiers having fallen victims to that dread disease, yellow fever.

The expedition left Brownsville with two cannons and provisions for several days. It took them three days to reach the enemy. They advanced slowly, with the greatest caution, sending men to reconnoiter, for they apprehended an ambuscade from behind every bush. Finally the enemy's fortifications are in sight. The expedition halts. Not one man is seen, no voice heard in the enemy's camp. Hearing of the expedition, had they left and crossed over to the Mexican side of the river?

Suddenly a tremendous volley of musketry revealed the situation. Quick as thought the Brownsville braves take to their heels, leaving one of their cannons behind them, which fell into the hands of the enemy.

The situation grew more critical every day. Cortina was receiving new recruits from both sides of the river. Every day at day-break the booming of the captured cannon seemed to say: "Brownsville come up and take me back, if you can!" thus setting the city at defiance.

It was on December 27, 1859, that the frontier was relieved of this desperate gang by the noble action of Captain W. G. Tobin, of San Antonio, who came down with sixty Texans and joined Col. J. S. Ford. Cortina and his men could not resist the combined forces of these gallant officers, who had come to rescue Brownsville and the frontier from the oppression and unrestrained lawlessness of ignorant and unprincipled men. Cortina was badly beaten and was forced to cross the river.

He afterwards became the Governor of the State of Tamaulipas, although his education was absolutely blank—for he did not know either how to read or write. Although expelled from Texas soil, his presence on the frontier still caused fear and terror. But the Federal government of the U. S. obtained from Mexico, his removal from the frontier. Forthwith he was sent to the Mexican capital under escort and kept there a life prisoner. He was, however, afterwards allowed some liberty, but obliged to present himself every day and report at headquarters.

Some years after these frontier troubles, three men who had participated in the Brownsville raid, were caught on the Texas banks of the river, arrested and sentenced to be hanged. To prepare them for the passage to eternity devolved upon me. For fifteen days I worked in vain endeavoring to bring them to repentance.

The day for the hanging came; I prepared to make the last assault and endeavored to have them realize their situation. "So you have resolved to go to hell?" I said, "but remember this: after you are hanged, you will fall into the eternal fire of hell, and at the first touch of it, you will exclaim, 'Oh, I could have escaped from it, but now I cannot!'"

"Father," said one of them, "please hear my Confession." After giving him the Sacraments, I said, "I thought that three would go to hell, but thank God, this one will go the other way and meet his merciful Savior." "Father," said the second, "is there any hope for me?" "Yes," I said, "even if your sins were one thousand times more grievous, if you repent and have confidence they will be forgiven you." "Hear my confession," he said. After giving him the Sacraments I repeated my words. "I thought the three would go to hell, but thank

God these two are already reconciled with God and men." Then addressing myself to the third one I said: "You rebellious soul, I abandon you to your fate; I am going to take my dinner; I shall be here at 2 o'clock to accompany you to the place of execution." "Father," he said, "have we time yet?" "Yes," I said, "God says at any time the sinner comes to me I will hear him and heal him." He also received the Sacraments.

While going to the place of execution, we recited the Rosary. Arrived at the gallows, the three knelt and received the last blessing. Mesericordias Domini in aeternum cantabo.

The venerable J. B. Vianney, the great winner of souls, a wonder of humility and mortification, the Thaumaturgus of the 19th century, was wont to say: "I am dealing with sinners every day of my life. Oh! when shall I be in the company of the Saints! If there were no heaven, how fooled I should be!"

Missionary life on the lower Rio Grande in those days, was anything but pleasant. Our lot was cast among outlaws and revolutionists from Mexico, seeking a refuge under the Stars and Stripes. Four Oblates in Matamoros, lived under the tyrannical rule of petty masters, subjected to all kinds of annoyances, except during the Emperor's short reign, when they enjoyed perfect liberty. Six Oblates in Brownsville were employed in parochial duties and the visit of numerous ranches.

Our Texas mission suffered chiefly from periodical revolutions in Mexico. Matamoros was generally the starting point for those who strove for the gubernatorial prize: Ruiz, Revueltas, Carvajal, Escobedo, Cortinas, Canales and a score of other Generals are notorious on the Lower Rio Grande. Revolutions were the order of the day. The Rojos, the Crinolinos, the Colorados, the Azules, were some of the appellations of the political parties of the time. The first question every morning was: "How many were killed last night?" Many a time our mission on the Texas side was blessed by the accumulation of the wounded and the vanquished, sometimes by revolutionists, concocting their schemes and plots; by robbers, and generally by the scum of our sister Republic. Our population was demoralized and our lot was cast in that pandemonium. Add to the above, that terrible plague, the yellow fever, which several times decimated our mission. Eleven Oblates fell victims to the terrific monster.

In those days of adversity and insurmountable difficulties, the Oblates quailed for a moment, and the mission was to be abandoned. The Cardinal Prefect of the Propaganda was advised of the project, and communicated the fact to his Holiness, Pope Pius IX. The following words came to us from Rome: "By order of the Pope, the Oblates must remain on that desolated frontier." Encouraged by the Vicar of Christ we continued our work of zeal and abnegation. The above was written by anticipation. I must now retrace my steps and take up the thread of my narration of episodes.

During the Confederate war, Texas seceded. The Federal troops land at Brazos Santiago. General Bee, the gentlemanly commanding officer of the Confederate forces at Brownsville, sets fire to the garrison; blows up the powder magazine and withdraws. The following day the Federals arrive, but find Brownsville deserted. We keep our post. We are now under Federal rule, and as gentle as lambs with our new masters. Shortly after their arrival, I was summoned to a sick call some twelve miles above the city. I applied to Major Starck for a pass. "No sir; I cannot give you a pass," said he. I forthwith went to General Heron, the commanding officer, to represent to him the urgency of the case. "Come back in about one hour," said he, "and I shall see that you get your pass." After waiting an hour I got my pass and then started for the sick call. On the road I met four different pickets of soldiers and was thus addressed by each: "Halt; were are you going? when do you expect to be back?" "Well, well," I said to myself, "I am certainly looked upon as a dangerous man or a spy."

A few years after the war, when Major Starck, who had become a citizen, came to see me. "Well, Major, said I, "are you going to get married?" "What makes you ask me that question," said he. "Because," said I, "when I asked you for that pass, you remember, your face was rather rigid, and now you are smiling." "Well Father, he said, "I will explain to you the reason of our conduct. When we arrived at Brownsville, we were told that the Priests were the staunchest adherents of the Confederacy. You remember the four pickets of soldiers you met on the road? We despatched them in front of you at equal distances, before we delivered you the pass. The enemy was only forty miles distant, and you were going in that direction, etc."

General Heron being satisfied that I was neither a suspicious character nor a spy, gave me a general pass. Major Starck married one of our best girls; his esteemed wife and family are still living in Brownsville.

A young lady one day came to see me. "Father," said she, "the Yankees have stolen my 600 goats; would you be kind enough to see the General about it and have my goats returned to me?" I forthwith started for the General's quarters. "General," said I, "some of your men have stolen 600 goats from a young lady, one of my parishioners." "I have no time to attend to such business," said the General, "I will refer the case to my military court." The following day I presented myself before the court. There was the prosecuting attorney, who asked me to state the case and endeavor to clear myself of what he considered an insult to the army. "For," said he, "you told General Heron that some of our men had stolen a number of goats." "Well," said I, "if you object to the word stealing, I withdraw it and say that some of your men have taken away 600 goats from the farm of a young lady: this is against the law of justice." "Do you not know that in time of war, we are allowed in strict justice to appropriate to ourselves the goods of our enemy wherever we find them? Our men, you know, have to be fed." "I understand your doctrine perfectly well, but, my dear sir, the young lady cannot be considered, and in fact is not, one of your enemies, for she is neutral." "Yes, but her father is a rebel." "That cannot be," said I, "for her father died fourteen years ago." "Is not Mr. Glavecke her father?" "No sir, he is her step-father." "Can this be proved by two witnesses?" "Yes, sir, immediately." Then I went in search of the two witnesses required by the court. They appeared and were sworn, and testified that the young lady's father had been dead for fourteen years. His Honor the Judge with a smile on his face said, "the 600 goats shall be returned to the rightful owner." And they were returned. "After all;" said I to myself, "there is fairness and justice among our friends, the enemies."

CHAPTER IV.

A Funny Interview. What Chewing Tobacco did. A Protestant's Remarkable Conversion. A Baby Baptized in the Nick of time. General Banks wants to study Spanish. A Poor Man Hanged. An Agreeable Surprise.

We are now under military rule, and no one is

allowed to leave the city without a pass. I shall continue my narration with a comical incident, which happened to one of our lay-brothers. He was greatly afflicted with stammering, and one day he was sent to cut some grass in a prairie a few miles from the city. "Brother," we said to him before starting, "provide yourself with a pass or else they will not permit you to go outside of the line!" His reply was: "M-m-me wa-wa-want n-no p-p-pass." He mounted his horse, and placing a long scythe on his shoulder, started off. On the road he met a picket of soldiers, and he relates the encounter thus: "O-o-one s-s-soldier c-cried h-h-halt, a-a-and m-me n-n-no s-s-s-scared a-a-and m-m-m-me t-t-told h-h-him m-me n-n-no b-b-bad m-m-man, m-m-me g-g-go c-c-cut g-g-grass, a-a-and the s-s-soldier s-s-said m-m-me, p-p-pass a-a-and g-go t-t-to g-g-grass." The following day he went with a Mexican cart to gather the grass which he had cut, and when passing in front of the picket of soldiers, he held up his Rosary before them and said: "L-l-l-look, t-t-this m-m-my p-p-pass."

Now to be serious. The streets were crowded, and our Confederate homes were either occupied by Federal officers or used for some of the various army offices. A large warehouse was used as a hospital for the privates, while a fine residence became the infirmary of the officers. Outside the limits of the city there were two more hospitals. At one time the number of patients was over 2000. A short distance from the city was an encampment of about 3000 colored troops, whose quarters resounded every night with loud cacophonic songs, as though 300 trombones were being used. At first my cassock attracted the attention of our new masters, for it is the custom of the Priests on the Lower Rio Grande to wear their cassocks outside the house as well as in it, and during visits to the ranches the cassock is found to be a good counsellor and protector. So our new comers had to become reconciled and accustomed to our special garb. Tobacco was scarce in those days, and the men would do almost anything to obtain it. Hence I used tobacco as a means to render my cassock popular. Through the generosity of Dr. C. Macmanus I obtained a good supply of chewing tobacco, which I cut into quids. When passing through the men I used to give them a quid of tobacco, and in a short time I became known as the Priest who gave tobacco. Soon both whites and blacks were wont to crowd around me, and my cassock became a pleasant sight for them, for they knew that its big pockets were well filled with tobacco. On the gulf shore at Brazos Santiago there was a military hospital containing two very large wards, where I was frequently called to attend to the sick. One day an Irish soldier sent me word to come down immediately to prepare him for death. I jumped on my horse with the determination of going straight to the sick man, but my horse took the wrong road, and being a little distracted at the time, I did not perceive this till the white houses of Clarksville were in sight. While there I proceeded to visit a small detachment of soldiers. As I alighted in front of Mrs. Clark's house, I was startled by these words from the lady:" "Father, go quick to that tent yonder, there is a dying soldier in it who is asking Almighty God to send him a Priest." I went immediately to the tent, and entering found the sick man lying on the bare ground. When he saw me, he exclaimed: "Blessed be God, who has heard my prayer." "Father," said he in a feeble voice, "I am going to die, and I have been praying very hard, asking God to send me a Priest, for I do not want to die a Protestant." I found the dying man well instructed in the Catholic religion. He had suddenly been ordered from the North to the South, on the very eve of the day appointed for his reception into the Catholic Church.

 I performed all the ceremonies necessary in such a case and then baptized him. When I told Mrs. Clark how I had come there by my horse taking the wrong road she exclaimed: "That was certainly an act of Divine Providence." I shall also relate another providential incident which, although of a later period, coincides well with the one above. One evening, while the community were taking their evening recreation, a man came for a Priest to go and baptize a sick baby some miles distant from the city. As the hour was already late I asked the man if the baby were in a critical condition, and he answered that the baby was not yet in actual danger. I then told him that I would go early the next morning. The man mounted his horse and was ready to start back, when the thought struck me, "what if that baby should die during the night?" I then told the man that I had decided to go immediately; I prepared my horse and started. We both traveled at a good gait and soon reached the house, where we were told that the baby was dying. I alighted as quickly as possible and went into the house, where I found that the baby was really in the pangs of death. I administered private baptism and while I was preparing my oil stocks, surplice, and stole, to supply the ceremonies, the child breathed its last. Some may ask the question, why do not the persons present baptize in such an emergency? Well they generally do, but in many cases their mode of administering baptism is null. For example, they say: "Joseph or Mary, I pour water on thee in the name of the Father and of the Son and of the holy Ghost," or in Spanish: "Te echo el agua en el nombre del Padre, etc.," which form is certainly null and void. But now you will say: "why not teach them the right form?" This is the very first thing the Fathers do when they visit a ranch, but it must be remembered that the Mexicans are generally nomadic. Many come from the wilds of the neighboring States in Mexico, they are here to-day and to-morrow leave for parts unknown, giving room to others of the same category.

But leaving the interventions of Divine Providence in worldly affairs, let us return to the interventions of men in the same sphere. When General Banks took command of the forces on the Rio Grande, he heard reports that the Priests of Brownsville had government property. So, one day, we had the honor of a visit from this renowned officer. He came, he said, for the purpose of taking lessons in Spanish and he was allowed to visit the house. He never came back to take his second lesson, but we received the visit of a detachment of five men, who asked permission to visit all the apartments of the house, which, of course, was refused.

Father Maurel, who was there with some other Priests, forbade the men to enter our rooms, which had been locked as a prevention and in prevision of what might happen. The sergeant then ordered the men to break open the doors. "We hold you responsible for this savage act," said Father Maurel. Whereupon they stopped, left our house, and never came back.

One day I received a communication from the General, ordering me to say prayers for the authorities of the United States on Sundays before preaching, and to say them just as they were said in the Catholic and Episcopal churches of the North. I sent the General the following polite and short answer: "General, perhaps you are not aware that with regard to divine worship, we owe obedience to our Bishop only. So, please do not request me to disobey my superior's orders." This ended the controversy. Another time the military authorities wanted to use our church as a military hospital. But upon my representation that, as it was a place for public worship and consecrated in an especial manner to that end, I hoped the authorities actuated by a sense of propriety would not disgrace themselves by rendering the church unfit for divine worship. They respected our church and did not carry that plan into execution.

A poor father of a family, a Mexican, had been drafted into the ranks and was stationed with his regiment at a place called Como Se Llama, some fifty miles from Brownsville. He felt very anxious about his family and asked permission to come down and provide for his children. But his request was refused; so he came down one day without permission and after arranging some family affairs was preparing to return to his regiment, when he was seized as a deserter and sentenced to be shot. He received the last Sacraments of the Church with perfect resignation and with lively sentiments of faith and contrition: offering up his life, as he said a short time before he was shot, for the sins of his past life.

Towards the end of the war we were again under Confederate rule. As is well known, the last engagement between the Confederate and Federal forces took place at La Tolosa, which is about fifteen miles from Brownsville. A small detachment of Federal soldiers had been left at Brazos Santiago to look after the goverment property. The Confederate forces at Brownsville were only a few hundred strong and it was reported one day that the Federal forces, being aware of the weakness of the Confederates, intended to march against Brownsville. When the Confederates heard of the intention of the enemy they marched out to meet the Federals half way. An encounter took place, and the Federals, about 200 strong, were obliged to retreat to

Brazos, having been repulsed by about an equal number of Confederates. This happened after the surrender of General Lee and the downfall of the Confederacy, but the news had not reached Brownsville at that time.

Shortly after the Civil War we were preparing a sacred concert and I chanced to go to Matamoros to distribute some programs. While there, I met the late Capt. Mifflin Kenedy in his office, and he asked me if that concert was to raise money. I told him that it was and he went to his desk and handed me a draft for $2,000 in gold, saying: "Father, this is to buy a chime of three bells for your church." I was so astounded at the generosity and magnificence of the gift, that I could not find words to express my gratitude. I merely said, "O Captain, what good news for Brownsville! Allow me to go immediately, and communicate this extraordinarily happy event to my fellow Priests," Then giving the Captain a warm shake of the hand, I departed. I had gone but a few steps along the sidewalk when he cried out: "Father, come back," Quick as lightning the thought flashed into my mind, that the draft was but a joke. When I returned to the office, the Captain received me with a hearty laugh and said: "Father, you have become so excited that you have forgotten your hat and cane," and in fact it was true; I had started for Brownsville, without either hat or cane. I was somewhat ashamed of this predicament and it was some time before my mind recovered its equilibrium.

The war was over, and now came the work of reconstruction. It took some time before we were readmitted into the Union; for, being Confederates, we were looked upon as inveterate rebels. Peace reigns on the Texas side of the Rio Grande. But there is trouble on the Mexican side. Matomoros is besieged: half of its population crosses the river, and Brownsville becomes the refuge of the frightened Mexicans, as on other occasions, Matamoros had been the place of refuge for the citizens of Brownsville. During those troubled times, the life of the missionary on both sides of the river was one of great labor and exceeding danger.

Now that peace reigned in Texas; the State went to work reconstructing its so called rebel citizens. We too were busy repairing the disasters brought upon us by civil war on one side and the revolutions on the other side of the Rio Grande. "The life of man is a warfare on earth" and "through many tribulations we must enter into the kingdom of God." The spirit of God is not for quietly sitting down and permitting the world to go as it pleases; is not one for despondency in the time of adversity. Nothing is more contrary to our progress, both spiritual and temporal, than trouble, vexations, crosses and trials, if not properly endured. To become downcast and lose heart in the time of misfortune reveals weakness, and a want of Christian fortitude. Worldlings know that discouragement is the harbinger of complete failure. A General who loses courage and becomes downcast after his first defeat, will certainly never succeed as a military leader; a merchant who is not gifted with a cool head and not prepared to bravely meet with reverses and adversity will soon come to both moral and financial ruin. A man who is crestfallen in the presence of his accusers is looked upon as guilty, though he be innocent. In any emergency we should keep a stiff upper lip, as is trivially said, and in the midst of prosperity be ever ready to meet a sudden stroke of misfortune. The Indians of Peru say," From happiness to misfortune there is only the leap of a flea."

CHAPTER V.

Terrific Cyclone. Convent Destroyed. The Sleeping Girl Saved. Four Thousand five Hundred Dollars Subscribed. An Impromptu Sermon. A queer way of Making Money.

But enough of moralizing! Let us return to the relation of facts and episodes. Our brave and devoted nuns of the Incarnate Word, when peace and tranquility were restored, saw that their institution was inadequate for the reception of the continually increasing number of pupils, so they devoted the earnings of fifteen years to the erection of an ample and costly addition to their original convent. This addition was two stories high and one hundred feet by forty long. At the same time a beautiful chapel forty by twenty-five feet was erected in front of the old building. Now our good Sisters were certainly entitled to enjoy the fruits of their labors for many years to come. Ample school rooms, music halls, studios for drawing and painting, well ventilated dormitories, and all requisites for a first class institution of learning were at their disposal. The good sisters were now enjoying the quiet of their cloister; the hammer and bustle of the workmen no longer disturbed the peace of their abode, and the work of enlarging their institution had received its last touch. The aspect of the future was certainly bright, when a dark and heavy cloud appeared in the North. When it burst, a strong wind arose and the rain poured down in torrents. Through the day the wind became stronger and stronger. In the evening it became more violent. The hammer was heard all over the city. The doors and windows were fastened and barred: everything forebode a terrible calamity. For three days previous an Irish woman had foretold the destruction of the twin cities, crying out in the streets, "Woe to Brownsville, woe to Matamoros!" She was looked upon as a crazy woman and locked up in jail as a disturber of the peace.

At 10 p. m. October 8th, 1867, a terrific hurricane shook the city to its very foundations. It seemed rather like a tremendous earthquake, which it would be useless to try to describe. Suffice it to say that the next morning the two cities were an unsightly heap of ruins. The prophetess of woe was killed under the fallen walls of the jail.

At day-break, I went out to survey the havoc made by the cyclone. My first anxiety was about the convent and its inmates. I found the new and costly building a heap of ruins, the chapel and the old convent terribly shattered and cracked: so damaged as to render them unsafe for habitation. At the beginning of the hurricane the nuns with their boarders had taken refuge in the chapel; where, with uplifted hands, they cried out for mercy and protection. One boarder was missing. Where was she? One of the Sisters ran up stairs and found the girl sound asleep in her cot. The child, 7 years of age, was wholly unconscious of the danger she had been exposed to. The Sister wrapped her up in a shawl and brought her safe to the chapel. One minute later, say the nuns, the dormitory, where the little girl had been found sleeping, came down with a tremendous crash. There is certainly a special providence for innocent souls.

The nuns, with their pupils were removed to St. Joseph's college, which had been spared by the fell destroyer. Here they continued the course of studies for a period of thirteen months. They were now without a house of their own, and without the means to build one. Still they did not lose courage nor become downcast. With renewed energy and confidence in God, who never chastises except to purify and prepare the soul for a more perfect work, they selected a new site and built a new convent, substantial, and as it was hoped: hurricane-proof. After a few years the heavy debts were wiped out, and as an act of gratitude, the good Sisters established a charity school on the lot across the street, and, in order to maintain the laws of the cloister, they built a closed bridge over the street: a franchise which they obtained from the city council.

Our church was saved from destruction by the exertions of Father Maurel, O. M. I., who, in the midst of falling bricks and beams from the tower, placed a ladder against the large window above the entrance door. Had this window been burst open by the fury of the wind, the church would have been doomed to complete ruin. The only damage done was the demolition of two turrets and the tower roof, which was carried off in one piece to a neighbor's yard, 200 feet distant from the church.

Nearly all the poor Mexicans' huts were down. A collection of $4500 placed in the hands of the Priests for distribution, helped considerably in rebuilding the poorest districts of the city. "Post nubila, Phoebus:" after clouds, sunshine. Six months had scarcely elapsed since the disaster, when the ladies undertook a big fair, which lasted four days. Three thousand four hundred dollars were netted, which was spent in the erection of the beautiful Gothic groined ceiling in our church. This was an epoch of progress. Several chapels were built at various points of our extensive mission. One day I was sent to visit a small district containing three of the above chapels, I spent the whole week out. Upon my return the following Sunday, I found the Father who had been detailed to preach at the High Mass sick in bed. The church was crowded. After brushing my boots and shaving myself, I ascended the pulpit and delivered an impromptu sermon, the text of which was, "Seek ye first the kingdom of God and His justice, and all these things shall be added unto you." After Mass there came to the vestry the Hon. Jerry Galvan, the wealthiest member of the congregation, who abruptly accosted me saying: "Father, you preached us a mighty good sermon. Could I buy some of those spiritual goods you mentioned in your sermon when you said, 'Lay not up for yourselves treasures on earth, where the rust and the moth consume, and where thieves break through and steal. But lay up for yourselves treasures in heaven; where neither the rust nor the moth doth consume and where thieves do not break through nor steal'?" "Mr. Galvan," I said, "if you wish to do something that will redound to the honor and glory of the church and to yours, give me enough of gold to buy twelve large chandeliers to hang from the ceiling of this church." "Yes," he said, "that would be the best ornament for your church; come and see me at my office to-morrow morning at 9 o'clock." The next morning I presented myself before His Honor, who handed me a cheque on London. I forthwith ordered the chandeliers to be made at the factory of Messrs. Poussielgues & Co., Paris. They arrived at Brownsville O. K. On our great festivals of Christmas, Easter, &c., when the 400 lights are lit up, the church presents a magnificent spectacle.

Our good ladies of Brownsville, always ready to help a worthy cause, volunteered to raise money to get a large pipe organ and I, to encourage them, tried an unwonted method to increase their exchequer. I got on my horse and, accompanied by four good shepherds, visited the wealthiest rancheros of the mission. In fifteen days we collected sixty-five cows, four horses and two colts. At the head of that herd I felt as proud as a

General returning home after a victorious campaign. You laugh, my friends, but I don't care; all my debts are paid off, and our organ is still pealing forth for the greater honor and glory of God, and I hope that it will continue to do so for many years to come.

CHAPTER VI.

Bishop Manucy. Reception. Sisters of Charity. Scribes and Pharisees. A Mob. The Bishop's Palm Sunday. His Good Friday.

The section between the Nueces river and the Rio Grande, which in the first quarter of this century was the paradise of the deer and the garden of the cactus and mesquite, commenced to be settled in the first days of the Republic of Texas and received a great impetus after the war with Mexico. Then the Republic became a star in the constellation of the American galaxy, and immigrants, especially from the neighboring land of revolutions, came in such numbers, that in the year 1874 the Holy See erected a Vicariate Apostolic in this southern portion of Texas. The first incumbent under the title Bishop of Dulmen "in partibus infidelium" and Vicar Apostolic of Brownsville was the Rt. Rev. Dominic Manucy. He was consecrated on the 8th of December, 1874; took possession of the Vicariate and was installed on the 14th of February, 1875. The feast of installation was truly grand. The people of Brownsville contributed $1,470 for the occasion.

At the first meeting of the ladies and gentlemen an outline of the proceedings for the reception and installation of the worthy dignitary was presented to the several committees for consideration. Mention was made of a grand procession passing under triumphal arches and through the principal streets of the city, of a throne to be erected in the church for the forthcoming Prince of the Church. The proceedings appeared in public print and evoked an anonymous letter to my address, containing the following sweet expressions: "Sir: I am delegated by the W. L. of W. M. G. R. P. A. O. of &c. (what these initials mean I am unable to say) to announce that if you attempt to have a procession through the public thoroughfares of our city there is a bullet ready for your worthless carcass and another for your d—— Bishop. And if you erect a throne for your d—— Prince of the Church........ (the d's prefixed above, perhaps, mean "Domine," Do you think so?) Remember, sir, that in this grand Republic there is no room for such trash as a Prince sitting on a throne. Bullets are in readiness, look out, &c." I pass over the rest through respect for my readers.

On the arrival of the Bishop, nearly the whole population went out to meet him. The cannon was booming, the church bells were chiming, the military band was playing a triumphal march when the Bishop came in front of the church yard. Two addresses of welcome were read; one in English and the other in Spanish.

A few days later, the installation of the Bishop was enthusiastically hailed by the population. It was indeed a triumph for the church of Brownsville. A large procession started from St. Joseph's College to the church, which was decked in festive splendor. Nothing occurred to mar the universal enthusiasm. The Bishop ascends the splendid throne erected for the Prince of the Church: no bullets so far.

A few days passed in peace and quiet, when suddenly there appeared in the local papers a most virulent article, signed W. M., and directed to the Bishop and to Catholics in general. This article contained the elucubrations of a morbid mind, and only expressed the sentiments of the few demagogues; Pharisees and scribes of the day.

At that time it seems that the press was in the hands of this clique, for the Bishop's reply was refused insertion, except by paying ten cents a line. But this was only the prelude to a drama that followed.

Twenty-two Sisters of Charity exiled from Mexico arrived in Brownsville on the 24th of February, 1875. The entire population sympathized with the poor Sisters. They were escorted from the steamboat landing to the church by the clergy and a numerous assemblage. It was 8:30 a. m. His Lordship offered the Holy Sacrifice of the Mass and delivered a most touching address, which brought tears to the eyes of the sympathizing audience.

The Sisters, invited by the Nuns of the Incarnate Word, made their home at the convent, where they remained until their departure for New Orleans, March 4th.

During that time several ladies came to see the Bishop, asking him to have compassion on the poor exiled Sisters and to receive them in his diocese. His Lordship answered that it was not advisable for the reason that he had no resources, and that, being a new comer himself, he did not as yet know the wants of the diocese.

The Scribes and Pharisees seized the opportunity to raise a mob. They worked in the dark, and on the day appointed for the Sisters' departure, 300 men appeared under the windows of the Bishop's appartments, vociferating and calling to the Bishop to come down The Bishop went down and confronted the mob, "My children," he said, "what is the motive of this gathering?"

"Bishop," said the spokesman, "we came to demand that the Sisters remain with us." "Are you all Cath olics?" "Yes, your Lordship." "Then as dutiful and obedient children of the Church, disperse immediately; obey your Bishop; go home and attend to your business. The sisters cannot remain; they have to obey their Superiors." The crowd dispersed at once like so many lambs. I stood by his Lordship during this short speech and can certify that he spoke with such determination, firmness, dignity and majesty, that the few words he said fell on those men like an electric shock. They were surprised, but not vanquished. It was said at the time that they had been hired by the clique to cause a disturbance and annoy the Bishop.

They forthwith, started for the depot, waiting there until the arrival of the Sisters. As soon as the latter had entered the car, the only passenger car attached to the train; the 300 men lifted the coach off the track with the Sisters inside and carried it to a distance of twenty feet from the track. The Mayor of the city, Mr. Parker, together with a large force of policemen, could not prevail on them to put the car back on the track; whereupon the Mayor came to consult the Bishop as to the best means to be used, in order to have the car replaced. The Bishop said to His Honor, who requested him to go and talk to the men himself. "No, Mr. Mayor, it would not be prudent on my part to expose myself to be insulted by those unprincipled and rough men; you had better go yourself and tell them that the Bishop promises them, that as soon as circumstances will permit, he will call the Sisters back, etc." His Honor returned to the depot, spoke gently to those ill-advised and misled men, telling them to put the car back on the track, so as to avoid the rigor of the law, etc. Forthwith, the 300 men placed the car back on the track, the engine whistled, and off went the train. There were over 3,000 people present to witness this strange drama.

But the trouble was not yet over. Gatherings of strange men, many of whom, it is said, were from Matamoros, caused alarm. Some ill-omened rumors were circulated in the city. Three persons were marked out as being the ones especially opposed to the Sisters remaining. During the day many warnings came to us from friends. His Honor, the Mayor, and the whole police force were prepared to maintain order during the night. An additional body of guards were stationed around the Bishop's quarters, and also around the college for my own protection. But as I was a "brave" man I ran away and hid myself. I put a Mexican hat on my head and donned a white coat, and under the cover of the night went to sleep in a jacal at a distance from the college. The next morning we were all found alive, and our foes had vanished with the darkness.

His Lordship in a letter to Bishop Quinlan of Mobile, to whom he related his splendid reception, together with the late episode, remarked: "I had my palm Sunday when the hosannas resounded all around me, it was soon followed by my Good Friday, when the "tolle tolle eum" was belched forth out of the foul mouths of a few Pharisees."

A few days after this dramatic episode, the Bishop took a pleasure trip to the neighboring ranches, where he for the first time saw the poor Mexicans in their primitive ways.

During Lent the Bishop delivered before a large audience, a course of very interesting lectures. The first subject treated was, "The Primitive Man;" the second was "Fallen Man;" the third, "Man Regenerated;" the fourth, "Means of Regeneration;" the fifth, "Confession," and the last, "The Holy Eucharist." These subjects were treated in a masterly manner and revealed the sound logician, the exact and learned theologian, and, at the same time, a man who had at his command the most appropriate words, to convey his ideas to the minds of his hearers.

CHAPTER VII.

The Mule's Tail. Up to the Hub. "Try, Try Again." "There She Goes." Bishop Hunting.

Bishop Manucy was a profound thinker, an interesting conversationalist, but a man who was somewhat melancholy and this made him unpleasant when under the influence of discouragement. It may be said of him what the famous St. Augustine said of many others, "his heart was restless until it settled in God."

In August, 1879, the writer of these reminiscences was sent to Corpus Christi, to accompany Bishop Manucy on a journey through at least eighty ranches, which had not been visited by a Bishop for many years.

Father Bretault, O. M. I., the missionary par excellence, had been previously dispatched to prepare the rancheros for the Bishop's visit. We left Corpus Christi about September 5th, in a heavy ambulance, loaded with ten or twelve boxes and trunks; the driver was an invalid Mexican, and the two mules, which were to draw us through the mud and sand for over two months, were in very bad condition. The whole equipment was so heavy that it would have required at least four mules to draw it, and an able-bodied driver to manage them.

We started, "in nomine Domni," and Father Booker, S. J., who had just preached a mission at Corpus Christi, cast a significant look on our equipage, and said with a wink of the eye: "I wish you good luck." "Arre," said our sickly driver, and a crack of the whip sent our mules a-kicking. We soon reached our first station, which was nine miles from Corpus Christi, and spent the night there.

The following day, after traveling about one mile, we broke down in the middle of a marsh. "What shall we do?" said the Bishop. "The best thing to do" said I, "is to send back to the ranch and get a couple of mules to pull us out." We did so, and to his surprise a negro came with one mule and a long rope. "What!" said the Bishop, "that mule will be of no use to us." His surprise was even greater when the negro unhitched the two mules from the ambulance, and then fastened the long cord to the end of the tongue of the wagon, and attached the other to the tail of his mule. "Are you crazy?" said the Bishop. "No, sah; I knows my business. Dis heah mule will land de whole business on the other side of de mud," said the negro with self-assurance. He mounted the mule; gave the beast a crack of his whip, and down went both in the mud. "Stop! Stop!" said the Bishop, "hitch on my two mules and put yours in front." "No, no, Bishop," said the negro, "dis heah mule am all right." So he remounted and gave the mule a vigorous stroke of his whip, and with one grand effort, the poor beast drew the ambulance from the mud. "My," said the Bishop, "I feared that the mule's tail was going to come off, but now I see that it is all right." "O, yes, Bishop, its all right; I knew it would be all right. Dis heah mule has been in dis heah business for many years and he has never lost his tail yet." During the trip we had many a laugh over the incident.

Three miles further on, we were bogged in the middle of another marsh. The mud was so soft that the wheels sank to the very hubs. "Now, now," said the Bishop, "what is to be done, Father?" The poor driver was an invalid, whom the Bishop had, through charity, engaged for the trip, and he was so feeble that he could not whip the mules. After repeated and useless efforts on the part of the driver and myself, we could not get the mules to advance an inch. I then took off my boots and stockings, turned up my trousers, jumped into the water, and began to unload the ambulance, so as to render it lighter. When this was done, I went behind to push the vehicle, while the driver urged on the mules, but all our efforts were in vain, for the driver was too weak and the mules knew it, and they were resolved to take things easy. Seeing this, I said, "Bishop,—salva reverentia,—take off your boots and come down behind the ambulance!" His Lordship put his dignity aside for a few minutes and came down into the mire and united his efforts with mine, but all to no avail. The vehicle did not move an inch. The Bishop said in despair: "Let us send back for assistance to the settlement, which we have just left, and let us return to Corpus Christi, and we shall continue this visitation next week, or as soon as the roads are in better condition." "But Bishop," said I, "it is impossible for us to postpone our trip, for Father Bretault is in the ranches below, making preparations for Confirmation. Moreover, I have told him that we should meet him at the first ranch of the Oblate mission, to make out our program for the visitation, and to postpone the trip now for eight days would render the undertaking a complete failure."

But the Bishop replied: "To advance is impossible; for the conditions of traveling are completely adverse to us, and it is absolutely necessary for us to postpone our visit until the roads become dry." To avoid such a result, I recommended the trying condition of affairs, in which we found ourselves, to the intercession of the Blessed Virgin Mary. "O Mary," said I, "you know full well the difficulties which surround us and how necessary it is for us to make this visitation; so aid us, by thy benign intercession. If we do not arrive on the appointed day, I fear that Father Bretault may become impatient and return to Brownsville." I then recited three Hail Marys in honor of the Immaculate Conception, and turning to the Bishop, I said to him: "Place your confidence in God, and say a short prayer to the Blessed Virgin Mary, asking her to aid us, and we shall conquer the elements." "My dear Father," said the Bishop, "your theology is correct, but it will not dry the roads." By this time, the Bishop had put on his boots and mounted into the ambulance. I did the same and then we recited our Little Hours. We had about half finished, when he put his breviary on his knees and exclaimed: "Father, do you not see something approaching in the distance?" "Yes," I replied, "that is a drove of cattle, with four men on horseback." We continued our office until the drove arrived; we then asked the cowboys to help us out of the mire, and two of them immediately hitched their horses to the tongue of our ambulance. In a few minutes the air resounded with the cracking of whips and expressions, which it would not do for me to repeat. But all their efforts were in vain; for, the ambulance remained as firmly fixed as ever, and finally the cowboys departed, saying that they could not remain any longer as they had to follow their drove.

"There now," said the Bishop, "did I not tell you that the only thing for us to do is to return to Corpus Christi and to remain until the roads become dry? But the question at present is, how shall we ever get out of this swamp before nightfall, as it is growing very late."

"Bishop," said I, "let us try again."

"Try again," said His Lordship, "when four animals and two strong men could not cause the ambulance to budge, how can you imagine that my poor driver and two thoroughly fatigued mules can succeed in removing it?"

"Well, Bishop, I will tell you what is to be done. Come down again and push with me behind the vehicle." The Bishop consented to do so for the second time; he took off his boots, went down into the mud, and placed his shoulder to the wheel.

We said three Hail Marys, the invalid driver whipped his mules, the Bishop and I pushed with all our strength, repeating at the same time, "Mary, help us." At last the ambulance moved. "There she goes," cried the Bishop, "whip up your mules, boy," and in a few minutes we were on the other side of the mud. The Bishop then recovered his natural good humor, never suspecting what was in store for him during the two following months.

About 5 p. m. on the same day, we arrived at a creek, which was greatly swollen and whose banks were very steep; for this reason we did not venture to cross over alone. So I went to a house, which was about one mile distant, to find some one who could inform us whether it would be possible to cross the creek or not. On entering the house I found three cowboys, who were taking a lunch. When I told them of our present difficulties, and previous adventures, one of them harnessed a good team and aided us to successfully cross the creek. We were then about eighteen miles from Collins, the next station, which we intended to visit. The Bishop asked the cowboy about how long it would be before we could reach our destination. To the Bishop's dismay he answered: "In case you are not bogged in the mud, you may possibly arrive there some time to-morrow." Fearing to meet with difficulties, if we endeavored to proceed alone, we hired the cowboy to accompany us. By applying his whips well and using words, which we could not understand and which are too unharmonious for pious ears to listen to, he so managed that we reached Collins about 9 o'clock the following night. The next day we went to San Diego, where we remained for a few days.

We set out from San Diego, accompanied by Rev. Father Jaillet, and went to the Concepcion Ranch, where the Bishop blessed a chapel. It was almost a daily occurrence for our coach to become stuck fast in the mud or some low marshy place, and for it to remain there until a team of oxen or horses could be obtained from some neighboring ranch to pull it out.

One of our great distractions during this laborious journey, filled with so many incidents, was hunting. It was in the month of October, and game was very plentiful. The Bishop had an old fashioned muzzle-loading musket, which he valued very highly; and whether it was due to the accuracy of the musket or the precision of the marksman, I can certify that during the two months of our journey, I hardly ever saw His Lordship miss a shot. Whenever any game appeared, he would tell his driver to stop the coach and then we were certain of having a savory morsel of some kind for our next meal.

One evening we arrived at a ranch, just about dark; the place was composed of about a dozen Mexican jacals. We immediately went to the jacal occupied by one of the best families, and asked the woman, if she could prepare supper for us. Her reply was, that she would do the best she could, but that she had not much to give us, as the only food which she had in the house were a few cold tortillas, (cakes made of pounded corn, soaked in lye.) These, we willingly accepted, because we had a good condiment to season them with, in the shape of a ravenous appetite. In the meantime, we remembered that the Bishop had killed about a dozen doves on the road, and we got the lady to roast some of them, and these, with the tortillas, furnished us with a delicious supper. The next question was where we were to sleep during the night. The only place available was a wicker and grass roof, supported by four poles. So that if we were to spend the night there, we should be the sport of the four winds. Father Jaillet went around the ranch looking for better accommodations, but none were to be found. Finally we were told that there was a school-house, which would be a fine place to sleep in; but the schoolmaster, who lived about three miles away, had gone home and taken the key with him. We sent a boy on horseback to his house, who soon returned with the key, and we spent the night in the school-house. The Bishop slept on a table about two feet shorter than his body, and Father Jaillet and myself on school benches. We could not sleep on the floor, because it was composed of a substance known as Mother Earth, and was exceedingly damp. When the Bishop placed himself on his short bed, he jocosely remarked: "It will go better now, for I have added two feet to it," meaning his own feet. We spent a miserable night, and many and varied were the exclamations which broke its silence.

Bishop Manucy said several times that he would be pleased to have all the happenings of this miserable journey written and forwarded to Lyons for publication by the Society of the Propagation of the Faith, in order that people might know what the Bishop and his Priests had to undergo while working for the salvation of souls in this poor diocese and be edified thereby. Four times our coach was stuck in the mud, and four times two horsemen providentially came to our aid. This is not poetry, but solid plain facts; some of those, who witnessed these events, are still alive and can bear testimony to the truth of what I say. One Sunday while the Bishop was going to a small ranch, about half a mile from where we then chanced to be staying, we passed by a lake and near it was a flock of curlews. Seeing them the Bishop exclaimed: "I hope those people we have just left behind will not be scandalized, but at all events we must have something to live on." So, bang! bang! went the musket and fourteen curlews were killed or crippled, and the Bishop walked knee-deep into the water to pick them up. But some were too far out and he had to send his driver for them. Our provisions were assured for the following day, as we had plenty of birds for ourselves and some to distribute amongst the poor people whom we visited. Up to this time the Bishop had shot about one hundred doves and other birds, some rabbits, and quite a variety of other game and many a time the game thus brought down by the Bishop's gun replaced the hard, stringed, sun dried meat used by many a poor ranchero. Never before had we seen such quantities of game, but, as I have already said, the season was favorable to us, for we were traveling during the months of October and November. After spending fifteen days or so in visiting the settlements belonging to the Mission of Corpus Christi and San Diego, we entered the district under the charge of the Oblate Fathers.

CHAPTER VIII.

Father Bretault.   A Lesson in Astronomy.
Rustic Scenes.   A Sight.

This portion of the Bishop's travels was very interesting and pleasant. The roads were in fine condition and the rancheros came from all directions to welcome His Lordship and to show their appreciation of his visit.

After visiting several ranches we came to one called Las Palomas and found everything in readiness for a solemn reception of the Bishop. Father Bretault, O. M. I., had gone there on the day previous to our arrival and begun to prepare the grown people for the reception of the Sacrament of Confirmation. A neat altar had been erected and decorated with a beautiful collection of wild flowers, which had been gathered by the good people of the ranch to adorn the altar as richly and tastefully as possible for the sacrifice of the Mass, which was soon to be offered up thereon. As we drew near this ranch we found quite a gathering of men, women and children awaiting us and in expectation of something exceedingly grand, but as to what it was to be they could hardly say.

The babies were present in this gathering and were giving a concert of their own, but with little regard to harmony and the smooth blending of sounds. The larger children looked with profound amazement at the Bishop's mitre and golden crosier, which were glittering in the sunlight. Some of them were even filled with fear and ran to their parents for protection, crying out: "He is coming! He is coming!" After confirming a number of grown up persons and children and bestowing his blessing on those present, the Bishop started for the ranch called Don Juan McAllen's.

Dona Salome, the wife of Don Juan, did everything which could possibly be done to render our stay pleasant "Now," said the Bishop, "we have reached civilization at last, this is truly an oasis in the desert through which we have passed." Here for the first time since he had set out on his journey the Bishop enjoyed a good sleep in a soft, clean bed. Rev. Father Jaillet now returned to San Diego, and since he had been our companion amid so many trying vicissitudes we missed him greatly. He must well remember how one night we slept in the Bishop's ambulance with the dome of heaven for a canopy. The stars twinkled in the firmament and recalled to our minds many of the astronomical lessons, which we had learned during our college days. We spoke about several of the planets and their movements, and were discussing the question whether or not Mars in its movement of circumvolution is at times as near the earth as Venus, when the rooster put an end to this discussion by vehemently announcing the Aurora. Father Bretault always went a day ahead of us to instruct those who were to be confirmed, and hear their confessions. On our arrival at the places which he used to indicate by saying, "I go North, South, East or West," we invariably found a list of the names of the persons whom he had prepared for Confirmation, written on a paper which he placed upon the altar, together with the indications of the road leading to the next ranch. Sometimes as we went along we had to stop at small ranches to confirm babies. Many persons who had not been to Confession for a long time, availed themselves of the Bishop's visit, to make their peace with God. Some of the newcomers whom we met, were from those districts of Mexico, where the word of God is seldom preached. They required considerable instruction before being able to approach the Sacraments properly. It was extremely difficult to ascertain when they had made their last Confession. To the inquiry, "How long is it since your last Confession?" the answers would be: "Since the coming of the Yankees;" "Since the siege of Matamoros by General so and so;" "Since the great fire;" "Since the yellow fever," and so on. Hence, if the Priest wished to know the time of their last Confession, he would be obliged to find out the time of these local events: by no means an easy task.

When we arrived at Los Federales ranch we were received with the greatest attention and display which we had yet witnessed during this journey, and I deem the conduct of the people of this ranch worthy of special mention. As we approached, several guns were discharged, to announce the Bishop's arrival. As we looked at the ranch from a distance we saw what appeared to be numberless flags, floating on the breeze, But as we drew near, we found out that they were but handkerchiefs attached to long poles which were arranged along the fences. A triumphal arch had also been erected and decorated with trinkets, flowers, and green branches. We found some of the women grinding corn, and others preparing tortillas under a large shed; a kid was being roasted over glowing embers; a large tent covered with hides, canvas, blankets, or some other pieces of strong cloth had been erected in the yard. Under this rural arrangement an altar had been placed, and a silk reboso (shawl), which had been worn 20 years previously by the landlady at her marriage, served as a canopy. The altar itself was decorated with a profusion of wild flowers and adorned with "santitos," (literally, little Saints) and other statues, which had been handed down as heir-looms from father to son and, though old and stained, were precious in the estimation of their owners and were looked upon as grand decorations by the Mexicans. The walls were covered with pictures of every kind, which had been cut from newspapers and fashion journals. A picture of General Jackson hung on one side of the altar and one of General Lee on the other. On the walls were pictures of steam engines, birds, horses, cows, sheep, and goats, and in fact papers representing nearly every animal contained in Noah's Ark. The four candles for the Bishop's Mass were stuck in four cups filled with corn. At last supper was announced, the table was spread beneath the tent and was laden with hot tortillas, roasted kid, baked chickens; eggs; hot coffee, and rich milk, in fact it was a supper fit for a king.

Father Bretault, or as he is called by the rancheros, "Don Juan de la Costa," which means "John of the Coast," because he had been for many years the missionary in charge of this district which was composed of 180 ranches, remained with us on account of the vast amount of work to be done at this ranch. When we had finished our supper; heard what Confessions were to be heard, and made the necessary preparations for the morning, we retired to a school-house where we were to spend the night. A comfortable bed had been prepared for the Bishop, but we poor Priests were left to our own resources. I saw an old cot lying amidst a pile of rubbish. After some manoeuvering I managed to repair it, so as to be able to stretch myself upon it. During the first part of the night the heat was quite oppressive, so I gave my blanket to "Don Juan de la Costa," telling him to place it on the bare bench where he had retired to rest. But for so doing I had to pay dearly, for at 2 a. m. a cold norther suddenly arose and I began to shiver like a poplar leaf in a stiff summer breeze, and there was "Don Juan de la Costa," comfortably wrapped up in my blanket. Some time after the arrival of the norther, he awoke, and discovering my situation, he began to joke me, saying, "Father, are you too warm, have you another blanket to throw over in this direction? If so, I can oblige you by receiving it." I saw that I had been caught, but all I could do was to grin and bear it. "Don Juan de la Costa" left us early the next morning to go ahead and prepare the next ranch for our arrival. The morning was cold, still the Mass in the tent was well attended. Silence and decorum reigned on every side. The tent was so completely filled that there was no room for pigs; dogs; roosters; kids, or other domestic animals. The only thing which disturbed the solemnity of the occasion was the lowness of the tent, which prevented the Bishop's mitre from observing a perfect equilibrium. We left this memorable ranch to continue the visit of smaller settlements, where work was abundant and food scant, because game had become scarce on the plains. After seventy days we reached the last ranch, where we accidentally found a young man who had severed an artery and was bleeding freely. We stopped the flow of blood by applying bandages. We then set out for Brownsville, taking the boy with us, and arrived there that same day. We immediately called in medical aid to save the boy's life. After eight days he recovered and we sent him back to his ranch, clad in a suit of new clothes and with two dollars in his pocket. He afterwards turned out to be a bad man and became the terror of the ranches. After spending fifteen days in Brownsville his Lordship went up the river, working as hard as his Priests: hearing Confessions and instructing the ignorant. During the entire visitation, that is, from Corpus Christi to Brownsville, and from Brownsville to Roma, on the Rio Grande, the Bishop confirmed 2,862 children and grown people. Many notable conversions took place during this time, and the Bishop's instructions everywhere produced a visible impression on his hearers. He acknowledged that never before had he witnessed such eagerness on the part of the poor rancheros to see a Bishop. "Life among them," said he, "is a little hard and food at times a little scarce. But thank God! my musket has supplied for any deficiency in food." "After all," said the Bishop, "St. Peter went fishing after he was called by our Saviour to the Apost late, and since this is so, could not a Bishop, even in the nineteenth century, be equally justified in hunting, especially, in that dreary part of his diocese where common food is scanty and the little which is to be obtained is unsavoury?" Be that as it may our pastoral visitation was remarkably blessed by Divine Providence. Great credit is due to Father Bretault, who for over twenty years has led a miserable life, humanly speaking, in that poor region and who has been doing a vast amount of good unknown to the world but which is recorded in heaven in the Book of Life.

CHAPTER IX.

The Right Rev. Bishop P. Verdaguer. Revisiting the Scenes of my Younger Days. Oh! Quam mutatus al illo.

The Vicariate Apostolic of Brownsville, after the appointment of Rt. Rev. D. Manucy to the See of Mobile, remained vacant for some years until the Rt. Rev. Peter Verdaguer of Los Angeles, Cal., was appointed Vicar Apostolic. I sent the happy news to a Priest at Los Angeles, who, among other encomiums, wrote the following laudatory words: "Father Peter is a zealous, pious man and an orator." It had been my pleasure, five or six years previous, to have made the acquaintance of Father Peter at Los Angeles, where I was his guest for a few days, and I willingly vouch for the truth of the above words.

His Lordship took formal possession of his Vicariate at Corpus Christi, but not long after he fixed his residence at Laredo. His reception at this place was so grand and magnificent, that had the President of the United States visited the city, a better reception could not have been given him. The religious, the civil and the military authorities mingled their joyous hosannas with the acclamations of a delighted and exultant people and rendered it a real triumph.

Since this memorable event, Bishop Verdaguer has built a good number of churches and chapels, and an hospital; formed new parishes, and all this with scanty resources. He has several times visited his Vicariate in all its nooks and corners. He is well liked by his Priests. "Ad multos annos."

Oh! when shall we see the long wished for iron horse traverse the immense plains of the lower Rio Grande; then such an impulse will be given to immigration, agriculture and commerce that the cacti and mesquites will give place to luxuriant cotton fields and sugar plantations. So be it. Such is the ardent wish of a former inhabitant and friend forever of the Lower Rio Grande and its people.

After forty-four years, I had the pleasure of revisiting, in company with Rev. Father McSorley, then Parish Priest of Beaumont, some of the places which I had visited during the travels of my younger missionary days, when Priests were scarce in Texas. I came to one of the portions of my former missionary labors, with the fond expectation of renewing many pleasing reminiscences of the days that are past and gone. And, how well I recalled the spreading plains, studded here and there with trees; the lofty pines beneath whose shade I so often sat and ate a piece of corn bread and a cold sweet potato; the pure air which I so often loved to breathe; the little feathered songsters which so often charmed my ears with their beautiful melodies! What joy it brought to my heart! The crane, as it raised its head above the high undergrowth and gave forth its dismal cry, reminded me that I was once more in the deep solitude, and at a distance from the homes of men. Still, I knew that God was near, and meditation was the natural outcome of my surroundings,, But now those distances, which were once so harrassing to the traveler, are traversed by the iron steed, which in a single hour covers as much ground as could formerly be covered in a day. Hail "Liberty!", the former home of a brave and noble race of Creoles; the Lacours, the Gillards, the Deblancs, the Blanchettes, etc., who now are dead, but whose children still remain, and possess the same characteristics as their forefathers. Their heads are already gray, and their forms are already bending beneath the weight of years. I met Jerome Deblanc: the sheriff, upon whom the flight of years had left its trace. He took us to his home, and as I related the events of former years, Rev. Father McSorley saw tears coming to his eyes. During breakfast an old lady about 70 years of age, asked me if I knew Father ——? "Oh yes, Madam," said I, "he is my best friend." But when I told her that I was Father —— himself, she rushed from her seat and embraced me. We visited two venerable ladies, whose heads were white as snow. They were two of the young ladies that sang at the First Communion of twenty-five children, whom I had prepared for the reception of this Sacrament during one of my missionary visits nearly half a century ago. Strange to say, we had dinner in the very same house where this ceremony took place forty-four years before. We were very pleasantly entertained by Judge D. and his amiable wife, who are the present occupants of this hallowed residence.

A strange circumstance was related by a lady, who learned that I was the Priest who had formerly visited that section of the country. It was as follows: One day in the month of February, 1853, I was traveling some thirty miles above "Liberty," where I lost my way and wandered about for an entire day and night. It was very cold and the ground was covered with an inch of snow, something unusual for that part of the country. At daybreak I saw a house in the distance, near the edge of a timber. Thither I directed my steps. I was cold, sleepy and hungry. A large dish of fresh pork was placed before me for my breakfast, but I refused to partake of it. The people were very much surprised, and were at a loss to know why I refused to eat of it. I told them that the day was Friday, and that it was forbidden by the Church to eat meat on that day. But I found the corn bread so savory and the sweet potatoes so palatable, that I consider that meal as one of ths best I ever enjoyed. The lady told me that from that day forth, meat had never appeared on the table on Friday, This caused me to say to myself: "Example is a powerful preacher."

But let us go to Beaumont. As the landscape looms up before me, how each memory of the past revives! How clearly I recall the spot, which I left early in the morning and to which I came back to it at evening! after wandering about the whole day. The city appears in sight! What a change! Is this Beaumont? The few shanties on the bank of the river Neches are nowhere to be seen. They have passed and gone, and upon their site there stands a beautiful city of 10,000 inhabitants. The Catholic church here is too small for its congregation, and near it stands a magnificent convent under the direction of the Dominican Sisters. The five weeks which I remained at Beaumont convinced me of the thoroughness of their system of education, and of the perfect discipline which they maintain. It requires a good amount of experience and tact to keep 200 children in perfect order during the entire time of study and recreation.

During one month we heard over 150 confessions in that place, where formerly I could hardly find a Catholic home wherein to spend the night. Still I perceived one stumbling block in the way of the Church's progress, a stumbling block which is universal—it is the falling off from the Faith of the children of mixed marriages, and the sad result of Godless education. Again, how many in remote places, which are not attended by Priests, have become apostates, and joined the nearest Protestant church! These and their children and their children's children are lost to the faith of their Catholic forefathers. The Catholic Church has made great progress, it is true; its churches, its Priests and its institutions have multiplied throughout the land, but if it had not such obstacles as I have just mentioned to contend against, it would number 20,000,000 instead of 10,000,000, as it does today. But withal the Church has fought a good fight, and it will continue to do the same until victory is perched on its banner. We shall now visit Orange on the Sabine River.

At the time of my first visit to this place, I found about twenty shanties, and only one Catholic—an Alsatian—who had lately arrived. He lodged me under his shed and cooked two eggs for me on a tin plate which he held over a lamp. This was the only place where I found nothing to do. I did not even administer a single baptism. During my visit I tried to locate the place where I had spent two nights with the Alsatian, but such changes had taken place that it was impossible. The whole neighborhood is now covered with beautiful residences. The lofty pine trees of '53 have all been turned into building material and only young shoots are to be found.

We shall now start for Galveston along the newly constructed road from Beaumont to Bolivar Point. As I passed along the route I recalled how on one occasion I started from Beaumont at 3 a. m., took breakfast at Sabine City, and arrived at Bolivar Point about 11:30

p. m., the same night. At that time there were no houses on the beach, but when I passed over the same route this last time I counted nearly 200 there. At the time of my first visit the only practical mode of traveling was on horseback, under a scorching Sun; and nothing could be found on the way but brackish water, with which to quench one's thirst. But traveling is easy now. There are plenty of coaches with soft cushions and the railroad accommodations are splendid. Yet travelers sometimes complain because there is no ice in the cooler, or chide the porter because he does not attend to their demands as readily as they wish. Since this is so, I wonder what they would do if they were obliged to travel over this route as others did forty-four years ago? Well, how the times have changed! "O tempora! O mores!" We spent two pleasant days at Galveston with the Rt. Rev. Bishop Gallagher, who was very kind to the "Old Missionary." While in Galveston, I visited the old frame house which had been the home of the good and saintly Bishop Odin. The sight of this old building brought back to my mind how on the 2nd of November, 1853, Dr. Jourdan had me taken from it to the new one at the rear of the Cathedral so as to remove me from the infectious atmosphere of the old one, where six Priests had already died from yellow fever. In this way I became its first occupant. On the 3rd of November I was taken down with this dreadful disease, and on the 5th I received the last Sacraments. I recovered rapidly, God reserving me for further works and troubles: "Per multas tribulationes."

PART IV.
FROM MEXICO TO ROME.
CHAPTER I.

Apparition of our Lady of Guadalupe. Authentic Documents. Aspect of The Miraculous Picture.

This will be the last part of the Reminiscences, and in it I shall speak of the items of religious interest, which fell under my observation during my voyage from Mexico to Rome,

Although Mexico is so rich in antiquities, beautiful in natural scenery, romantic in history, venerable in ruins, and luxuriant in its tropical vegetation, I shall not describe any of those, but shall confine myself to its religious phases. The same will be done in regard to Rome..

The most stupendous events recorded in the history of any nation are revelations and apparitions from Heaven. The Old Testament is replete with the records of events of this nature. The New Testament opens with a reference to the apparition of the Son of God made man:

"And the word was made flesh and dwelt amongst us."

As the ages passed, His Blessed Mother also appeared at various places and times to remind man of his sublime destiny. The grandest and most illustrious event of this nature in the history of Mexico is the apparition of our Blessed Lady on the Tepeyac near the City of Mexico.

From all the narrations of this apparition I have selected one published in 1649 in the Nahuatl language by Father

Luis Larra de la Vega, who found it in a manuscript written a century previous, and for this reason it is almost contemporary with the event itself. The authentic document itself is to be found in the archives of the Collegiata of Guadalupe. It was translated into Spanish, by the able historian Boturine. Although the narration is long, I prefer it to many others of a later date, for the reason that the more contemporary a document is the more reliable it is. This will possibly be the first time that this document has been translated into English:

1. Herein it is related and explained how the illustrious Virgin Mary, Mother of God, Our Lady, lately miraculously appeared in a place which is called Tepeyac.

2. She appeared directly to a native called Juan Diego, and indirectly through an apparition of her sacred image to Father Don Juan de Zumarraga, first Bishop of the City of Mexico. Many miracles are said to have taken place. Ten years after the work of introducing water from the mountain into the city, Mexico began to grow; peace dawned in every part; the light and knowledge of Him, who is the author of life and the true God, began to shine forth and become manifest.

3. In the beginning of the month of December 1531, a poor native, who lived in Quahutitlan and belonged to the district Tlaltelolco, where he was instructed, early one Saturday morning as he approached the hill called Tepeyac, heard the singing as it were of many birds, the echo of whose voices resounded from every side.

4. Juan Diego instantly stopped and listened to the joyous songs and said within himself: "Is this a dream? How enchanting! Is this the terrestrial Paradise spoken of by our ancestors?"

5. He was looking in admiration towards the top of

the hill whence came the songs, when suddenly they ceased and he heard a voice calling, "Juan;"! and Juan Diego remained stupefied.

THE FIRST APPARITION.

6. Recovering from his emotion, he went up the hill whence the voice came. When he reached the top he saw a lady whose beauty was beyond his comprehension. Her dress was as brilliant as the Sun. Everything around her was as resplendent as the purest gold and more beautiful than the rainbow. He bowed reverently and heard the following words:

7. "My beloved son, Juan! Where are you going?" He answered: "I am going to Tlaltelolco in Mexico, to learn the divine truths which our Fathers are teaching there." The Lady added: "My son, my protegee; know that I am the Virgin Mother of the true God. He is the Creator of heaven and earth. My ardent desire is that a temple be erected on the spot which I shall point out to you, and where those who invoke me will find out how I love them and how I shall aid them in their wants. I shall show them that I am a tender mother to them; but in order that this may be accomplished, go, my son, to the palace of the Bishop of Mexico and tell him that I myself sent you to make known to him my desire of having a temple erected here. You may tell him all you have heard and seen. Go, my son, and to show my gratitude toward you I shall obtain for you the reward of eternal glory."

8. Juan immediately prostrated himself at the feet of the Virgin and exclaimed: "I shall go, my Lady, and I shall do exactly as you have requested me to do."

9. He set out for Mexico and directed his steps towards the Bishop's palace. When he arrived, he told the servants to inform the Bishop that he wished

to speak to him. The servants, seeing that he was a poor Indian, did not pay much attention to him and he was obliged to wait for a long time at the door. Finally the Bishop beckoned to him to come in. Juan Diego immediately fell upon his knees and related to the Bishop how he had seen the Queen of Heaven; repeated the words which he had heard from her lips, and made known the message which she had confided to him. The Bishop hardly believed what the Indian had told him, yet he said to him:

10. "My son, you must come back again; I must hear you again in order that I may examine into the matter from the very beginning." Juan went out, quite sad, because the Bishop would not believe his message.

THE SECOND APPARITION.

The Indian left that same day and went straight to the same hill; where he again beheld the Queen of Heaven on the very spot where she had appeared to him before. Juan, when he saw the Virgin again, threw himself flat on the ground and exclaimed: "O my Lady! my noble lady, I delivered your message and I was received with difficulty, and finally when I was admitted into the Bishop's apartment, I delivered my message in the same words in which you expressed it to me. He received me with benignity and listened to me with attention; still he told me that he did not believe me. However, he requested me to return at another time as he would be pleased to see me again and to examine into my message from beginning to end. According to what he told me I understand that he considered that the temple, which you wish to have built here, was but an imagination of mine. I beg you, my Lady, to send some of those great men who are known and revered, and they will deliver your message and be believed. I am a poor man and for this reason unworthy to go where you sent me. Forgive me, my beloved lady, and be not angry with me."

12. The ever noble Virgin answerd: "Listen to me, my beloved son. I have other ambassadors who could carry my messages and give testimony to the truth of my wishes. But this thing is in your hands, and it is my wish that you go yourself tomorrow and see the Bishop, and inform him that it is my wish that a temple be erected here. Tell him once more that I, the Virgin Mary, Mother of God, send you." Juan Diego replied: "My kind Lady, Queen of Heaven, be not angry, for with all my heart I shall again repeat your message. I do not refuse to do so once more; I merely feared that I should not be listened to. I shall give you an account of my mission."

13. After these words he set out for his home. The following day, which was Sunday, Juan went to Tlaltelolco to hear Mass, and immediately after his devotions, he started for the Bishop's palace. He had the same difficulty in being admitted as before. He fell on his knees; wept bitterly, and gave an account of his mission from the Queen of Heaven.

14. Many were the questions which the Bishop asked the poor Indian. "Where did you see the Lady? How did she look?" Juan related all he had seen and all he knew about the affair. He spoke plainly and asserted that the Lady was truly the Immacculate Virgin, Mother of God. The Bishop refused to believe him, adding: "Your word is not sufficient proof. If the Lady be truly the Mother of God, go and request her to give you a sign by which I may certainly know her to be such."

15. Juan Diego replied: "Bishop, what kind of a sign do you wish me to obtain of the Virgin; I shall go at once to ask for it." His Lordship seeing that the Indian was in earnest, told him to go and bring him a sign. At

the same time he sent some of his servants to watch the Indian and see to whom he was going to speak. Juan started at once and the Bishop's servants followed him at a distance. When they arrived at the bridge built over the creek which runs at the foot of the Tepeyac, they lost sight of the Indian; they searched for him in every direction, but were unable to find him. They grew impatient, angry, and returned to the Bishop's palace. They told his Lordship that the Indian was a fraud, an impostor, and that they had decided to seize him and chastize him were he to call again.

16. The following day, Monday, which was the day appointed for Juan to bring the promised sign to the Bishop, he failed to appear for the reason that when he returned home he found his uncle Juan Bernardino very sick with a burning fever. The next day, Tuesday, finding his uncle in a critical condition, he ran to Tlaltelolco to request one of the priests to come and administer the last sacraments to his uncle who was in great danger of death.

17. When he arrived at the Tepeyac hill, he changed his route saying to himself; "If I take the path I followed the previous days, undoubtedly the Lady will see me, and cause me to lose time by giving me the sign required by the Bishop."

18. Juan went up by the other side of the hill in order to avoid a meeting with the Lady and said to himself: "She cannot see me here."

THE THIRD APPARITION.

Suddenly he saw the Queen of Heaven coming down from the top of the hill, and approaching him, She said to him: "My son, where are you going?" Juan frightened and blushing, fell prostrate to the ground and said: "Oh, my Lady! how are you, mi Diosa; mi xocoyota;

Dios te guarde; your heart will grieve when I tell you that my uncle is grievously sick and is going to die, I am hastening to Mexico to get a Priest, permit me to fulfill my mission, and I will return to-morrow.

19. The Virgin kindly listened to Juan, and when he had finished making excuses, said, "My dear son, do not be excited, do not fear; be of good heart; am not I your Mother? Heed not your uncle's infirmity, he will not die, he will recover and become as hale as ever." (It was known afterwards that Bernardino was cured at that very hour.)

20. Juan Diego was delighted and consoled when he heard these words from the Queen of Heaven, and he asked her to give him the sign which his Lordship required as a proof of the truth of his message. The Virgin then said to him: "Go, my son, to the top of the hill where you saw me before; there you will find a variety of flowers; cut them and bring them here to me."

21. Juan obeyed and was surprised to find such beautiful flowers and Roses of Castille at that season of the year, and on that sterile spot. So great was their fragrance that the entire mountain was perfumed by them. The Indian immediately began to gather the flowers and to place them in his tilma (a kind of mantle). When he had filled it, he went down the hill and presented them to the Queen of Heaven, who took them in her pure hands, put them back in the Indian's tilma, and said to him: "My beloved son, go to the Bishop, and give these blossoms to him in my name, and tell him that they are the sign which I send to him as proof of the truth of your message regarding the church which I wished to have built on this spot."

22. Juan started at once for Mexico, but when he arrived at the Bishop's palace he found all the servants indisposed towards him; they made him wait for a long

time at the door; they even insulted and struck him, and only ceased when they beheld roses in his tilma, for they were surprised to see such beautiful flowers at that season of the year, and they were even more surprised at the sweet fragrance which they emitted.

23. When the Bishop heard the confusion, he came out of his apartment and beckoned to the Indian to enter. Juan gave a lengthy relation of all that he had heard and seen.

APPARITION OF THE MIRACULOUS IMAGE.

He then spread on a table, the beautiful flowers which he declared he had plucked, at our Lady's request, from the bosom of a barren rock. It was while in the act of delivering these miraculous blossoms to the still doubting Bishop, that a greater miracle took place. A flash of supernatural light revealed to the prelate a picture of the Queen of Heaven herself, sketched upon the mantle of Diego. Falling down in veneration before it, the Bishop vowed his life to the fulfillment of Our Lady's mandate. (This precious cloak was placed in his oratory. The picture is wrought upon a course textile fabric and appeals alike to the eye of faith and to the eye of artistic appreciation.)

24. Juan Diego remained that whole day in the Bishop's palace. The next day he started for his home, accompanied by several men who were sent by the Bishop in order that they might see and inspect the place where the Queen of Heaven had appeared, and also to pay a visit to Juan Bernardino.

When they entered the home of Bernardino they found him in good health. Juan Diego revealed the circumstances of the apparition and of his visits to the Bishop, when suddenly Bernardino exclaimed that he also had seen the Queen of Heaven who had cured him of his infirmity and told him that he also must go to Mexico to see the Bishop. At the same time the Queen of Heaven told him that the Holy Image was to be called SANTA MARIA DE GUADALUPE.

25. Bernardino was brought into the presence of the Bishop to whom he related under oath, all the circumstances connected with the above facts. Juan and Bernardino then remained in the Bishop's palace for a few days. In the meantime the Holy Image was transferred from the Bishop's oratory to the Cathedral, that all the people might see it.

26. The whole city was aroused and ran to the Cathedral to see the Holy Image painted not by the hand of man, but by that of the Mother of God on the mantle of Juan Diego, which mantle was woven with ayate (a kind of stuff manufactured out of the thread of the agave).

27. This ayate mantle on which was imprinted the Sacred Image of the Immaculate Virgin is composed of two pieces joined together with cotton yarn, and its length is about "seis cuartas y una cuarta de muger,"— about one yard and three quarters.

Here ends the relation of Luis Lasso de la Vega in 1649, translated in Spanish from an old manuscript, almost contemporary with the event. In the above translation I gave the substance of the document, and avoided many repetitions found in the original which add nothing to the clearness and trend of the subject.

The picture is wrought upon a coarse textile fabric and though 366 years old, retains its original freshness of colors and strength of outline. An examination of the garment shows no difference in fashion or material from the cloaks or blankets usually worn by Indians of Diego's days and nation; but no test to which the painting has ever been submitted can reveal by what medium the celestial artist's hands transferred the holy outlines to such seemingly rude canvas. It is neither distemper, water color nor oil.

The beholder is astonished by the grace, tenderness and dignity of the picture. Clothed in a sunlike garment and wrapped in a mantle embroidered with stars, the majestic yet benign figure stands upon the crescent Moon in exquisite pose, and the hands are clasped as if in prayer, upon the breast. Even those who have no belief in the miraculous origin of the picture can hardly look upon it without a deep religious impression. So attractive is the charm of the blended sweetness and majesty of the picture, that no one can wonder at the ecstatic love with which the Mexicans gaze on the image of her, who appeared to one of the poorest of their race, and impressed her radiant likeness upon his blanket as a marvel and token for all generations.

CHAPTER II.

Office Approved by Benedict XIV. New Office Approved by Leo XIII. Two Distichs by the Pope. Indian Festivities. Maguey. Pulque. Mescal.

The proofs of the wonderful apparition of the Queen of Heaven are so numerous and convincing that no doubt can reasonably be entertained regarding their authenticity.

In each order of proofs there is an irresistible convincing criterion of their truth. In the historical order, there are the contemporaneous records of the fact. In the monumental order there are the Colegiata; the churches, and other monuments erected in commemoration of the event. In the traditional order there are the decisions of all the prelates of the Mexican church. In the religious order there is the history of the cult rendered to the Queen of Heaven under the invocation of our Lady of Guadalupe.

The Holy See: the highest authority in the world, has approved a special Office for the Feast, and Benedict XIV himself composed the prayer for the Mass of Our Lady of Guadalupe, and Leo XIII ordered a new Office for the Feast, with the fourth, fifth and sixth lessons of the second Nocturn containing the narration of the apparition. His Holiness also composed two distichs in honor of Our Lady of Guadalupe. I give them as they were written in Latin, together with a Spanish translation by the Archbishop of Guadalajara:

Mexicus heic populus mira sub imagine gaudet
　Te colere, alma Parens, praesidioque frui.
Per te sic vigeat felix, teque auspice, Christi
　Immotam servet firmior usque fidem.
　　　　　　　　　　—Leo. P. P. XIII.

(Imagini augustae Mariae D. N. Guadalupensis in Mexico subscribendum.)

Romae, ex aedit. Vatic. die XXVI febr, an, MDCCCVC.

Spanish translation:
　　En admirable Imagen,
　　O Santa Madre nuestra
　　El pueblo Mexicano
　　Gozosa te venera,
　　Y tu gran patrocinio
　　Con gozo y gratiud experimenta.
　　Feliz y floreciente
　　Porti asi permanesca
　　Y mediante auxilio
　　Que benigna leprestas
　　La fe de Jesucristo
　　Fija, conserve con tenaz firmeza.

The literal English translation is:

"In this wonderous picture, O Holy Mother, the Mexican nation reveres thee, and joyfully experiences thy protection; happy and flourishing under thy aegis may they be constant and firm in the faith of Jesus Christ."—Leo P. P. XIII.

In every city, town, village, hamlet, hacienda and rancho, there is either a church, a chapel or an altar in honor of Our Lady of Guadalupe. In a word, in almost every house of the Mexican Republic you will find the traditional picture of her apparition.

The devotion to Our Lady of Guadalupe has received a still greater impetus by the fact of the coronation of the Sacred Image, ordered by His Holiness Leo XIII. One of the greatest of the literati of Mexico said: "Mexican nationality is doomed on the day when devotion to the Virgin of Tepeyac ceases."

Previous to the Feast of Guadalupe, which takes place on December 12, the Indian tribes have each, a day appointed for their celebration in honor of Our Lady of Guadalupe. On the days selected by the ecclesiastical authorities, each tribe comes led by its chief. As they arrive they may be seen carrying on their shoulders immense wheels loaded with pyrotechnics; all kinds of musical instruments, of their own make, and everything necessary for the celebration of the day. Every one carries something. Babies, bags, boxes, fruit, corn, etc., are carried on the head or back. The little children are carried on the shoulders of their mothers, and are supported by their reboso or shawls. When everything has been unloaded, the women take charge of the food, and the men attend to the placing of the wheels for the pyrotechnic display. This being done, they all march to the church to assist at solemn Vespers. At night the fire works are splendid. The following day the whole tribe assists at Mass, after which comes the traditional dance called Matachines. In this ceremony they dance; bow to the Virgin, kneel down, pray and sing. All this is done in the sanctuary in honor of Our Lady of Guadalupe.

On the 12th of December, I left for Puebla. As the train passed in front of the sanctuary there were over 25,000 people in the plaza. We passed Otumba where Cortes won the miraculous victory over 200,000 Indians!

About half way from Otumba to Puebla is Apam, celebrated for its pulque, which is considered the best in the Republic. I shall briefly explain what pulque is. There is a wonderful plant called the maguey or "century plant." It is said that there are thirty varieties of the plant. It flourishes best at an elevation of about 7,000 feet. At this elevation miles of maguey plants may be seen. In its numerous leaves, often eight or ten feet long, a foot wide, and half a foot thick, its stores its sap for ten or twelve years and finally produces its flowers and dies. This flowering is prevented by cutting out the heart and stem of the plant. The reservoir thus formed at the base of the great leaves receives the sap, and this sap is gathered by the Indians. It is sweet, and hence it is called agua miel (honey water.) After a process of fermentation, it becomes pulque. By distillation, a liquor is obtained, called mescal, which is very fiery and intoxicating. It is pronounced to be the best remedy for incipient consumption, and pulque for diabetes. As I have said, pulque is the fermented sap of the maguey. Tequila is simply a brand of mescal. A famous hacienda named Tequila, produces the best mescal, and for this reason almost all mescal is called Tequila just as almost all cigars are called, Havana or brandy, Cognac.

CHAPTER III.

Puebla on December 12. Splendid Scenery. Misa de Aguinaldo. The Pastores.

Leaving Apam we arrived at Puebla at 12 a. m. All

the church bells of the city were chiming and the streets looked like so many profusely and admirably adorned churches on account of the number of altars erected in front of the houses, and the bunting; streamers, banners and flags displayed. The pictures of Our Lady of Guadalupe were seen hanging from every balcony, or in tastefully adorned windows, and there were many mottoes like these: "The city of Puebla to her Patron Saint," "Guadalupana bless our home." Bands of singers were heard in every corner, singing alabanzas in honor of Mary Guadalupana. Bands of music and orchestras were playing all over the city. The City of the Angels, as Puebla is called (Puebla de los Angeles) resembled an immense cathedral on the 12th of December, Feast of Guadalupe, Patronal Feast of all Mexico, rather than a mart of commerce.

A few days after my arrival I went to a country church about four miles from the city, where a "funcion" was celebrated. The church was so crowded that I found it impossible to enter either through the large front door or the sacristy. I met a Priest, who like myself, was unable to gain admission. "Padrecito," said he, "if we cannot get in, let us go on the roof." A stone stair-case leading to the flat roof, was soon climbed. There we stood. Beneath our feet we heard the solemn singing of the Vespers, interrupted at times by an occasional cantata accompanied by an orchestra. The view from this elevation was so grand and picturesque, that it still remains fresh in my memory. In the West, the setting Sun lit up with gold the summit of the huge Popocatapetl, while in the East towered high the snow-capped peak of Orizaba, and in the South, a luxuriant and fertile valley extended as far as the eye could reach. At last the bells rang for the Benediction of the Blessed Sacrament, and we knelt down in adoration of the Omnipotent God of Nature and the Eucharist.

One day in company with a Lazarist Father, we visited the Church of St. Francis and the adjoining garden, the property of the Bishop, situated in one of the suburbs of the city. There I perceived an apple tree loaded with fruit; yielding to the temptation I ate forty apples in a very short time. I hear some exclaim: "Horror! Did you get the cholera?" Not at all, and if the bells had not called us to the church, I could have eaten double the quantity. I had never seen such a diminutive apple in my life; about the size of a small cherry.

Nine days before Christmas, the Misa de Aguinaldo is celebrated at 3 o'clock a. m. in all the churches in Mexico. Every day for nine days, crowds are gathered at that unusual hour to assist at the Mass of the Infant Jesus. Led by curiosity as much as by devotion, I assisted at one of the Masses. A splendid orchestra preluded and the Office commenced. At the "Kyrie" there was a burst of enthusiasm, a real explosion, which caused me to exclaim in surprise: "Hello! what is this?" to a neighbor Priest. "Padrecito," said the Priest, "they are the birds announcing the coming of the Child Jesus." What was it? Nearly every member of the congregation, not only children, but men and women, were furnished with a whistle, and at the "Kyrie, Gloria, Sanctus, Agnus, &c.," there went the explosion of 500 or 600 whistles accompanying the organ and the singers. One day during the Novena I visited another church, where I saw near the entrance of the sanctuary four personages, life size, dressed as travelers, with white straw hats on their heads. These were the Blessed Virgin Mary, St. Joseph, one man holding a drum and the other a violin. On Christmas morning I visited the same church in order to see what had become of the four travelers. They were attired in festive clothes, but their hats were off.

The Infant Jesus was upon the altar, and the four were prostrate in adoration around it.

It is known fact that the Franciscan Friars who carried the Catholic religion into Mexico, seeing that the Aztecs were fond of solemn rites, glittering shows and mysterious ceremonies, instituted a series of religious plays and scenes drawn from the stories of the Bible.

One of the most remarkable performances is that of the "Pastores," which is still dramatized about Christmas in the Mexican Republic and on the American side of the Rio Grande.

The drama is admirably described in the "Gulf Messenger," by Miss Cordelia Fish Brodbent, who so vividly represents what I have seen rendered by the Mexicans, and read in two printed copies in Mexico, that I insert the following extracts:

"As we sit musing and comparing we hear the faint tinkling of bells, which becomes clear and more distinct as the "pastores," led by Mary and Joseph, march into the courtyard two by two, singing in soft musical voices:

> "Volemos pastorcitos,
> Volemos con violencia!
> Que en el portal esta
> La grande Omnipotencia.
>
> "Let us fly, dear shepherds!
> Let us fly with swiftness!
> For on the porch there is
> The great Omnipotent.

"Their costumes are unique. Mary wears a blue dress; a light blue mantilla spangled in gold and silver falls over her body, while a golden half circlet rests on her forehead to represent the halo surrounding her head, with which the great masters generally honor her. Joseph, with a dark blue tunic, and a long blouse of corresponding color, with gilt bands on hem, sleeves and neck, appears with a golden crown on his head and a staff of many colors in his hand.

"Back of these come the two angels Michael and Gabriel, the former in a blue tarleton dress, with golden wings and crown; and a sword at his side, while the latter is dressed in pure white, a wand composed of white flowers in his hand, and with golden crown and wings.

"Then follows the gila (shepherd's cook) in ordinary dress, very much bespangled, and a shepherd's crook in her hand. She is accompanied by the Priest, who is robed in the ordinary dress of to-day. The next in line hold our attention. They are the pastores (shepherds) and the principal actors of the evening. Their clothes are ordinary, but their crooks (ganchos) and lunch baskets (alforja) require particular mention. The crooks are five feet long entirely covered with paper of every color, and on the top, instead of one hook, there are four hooks which come together, having the appearance of a crown. This crown is also covered with colored paper, while bright ribbon streamers give them a gay and gaudy appearance. Inside the crown of the crooks are suspended many small bells. These staffs are struck on the ground to keep time with the music, and consequently the jingling of the bells is added to the melody of their songs. The lunch baskets are small—about eight inches long by four inches deep—and are trimmed to correspond with the crooks, being suspended from the shoulders by bright-hued streamers.

"After the chorus, upon entering, the first act opens with the meeting at the temple of the patriarchs, who have assembled to elect a husband for Mary. Fortunately, from the inference drawn as the play advances, though she had no voice in the matter of selecting a husband, the election exactly suited her taste.

"The shepherds open this act with the Crier's Call, and sing in loud voices:

> "Ocurran todos al templo
> En este dichoso dia!
> Para ver quien es elejido
> Esposo de Maria, etc.

> "Proceed all to the temple
> On this auspicious day!
> To see who will be elected
> To be husband to Mary, etc.

"After the election of the husband, Mary and Joseph appear together, come forward and kneel down before the Priest who meets them in the center of the square and performs the marriage rite. Hardly have the last words of his blessing descended upon the two, when the entire company come forward and join in songs of merriment and rejoicing. The feast is spread and all are gay and happy, unconscious of the presence of the dark, sinister figures off at one corner, who are looking upon the scene with perturbed countenances.

"There is a commanding form with dress of sable hue. He wears knee breeches with large buckles at the sides, hunting boots, a round cloak over his shoulders, and a black cap with two black plumes. A few spots of gilt illumine this sombre attire, and at his side a sword hangs in its scabbard. He wears a black mask with the face of a lion and two long horns protrude from under his cap. This is Prince Lucifer with his imps Satan, (Satanas); Sin (Pecado) and Leviathan (Leviatan). These imps are in sombre black, nothing relieving its intenseness, and with the exception of Satan, who is sometimes burdened with a very long tail made entirely of fire-crackers, their suits are exactly alike. This tail of Satan is set on fire when Lucifer and his imps are banished from earth (a ludicrous imitation of thunder, smoke and sulphur).

"As the merry-makers disappear Lucifer comes forward and draws his imps around him. He announces to them the fact that it has come to his knowledge that a maiden is to give to the world a Redeemer of mankind. He tells them that the prophecies of Ezekiel are accomplished, that he has read the signs and that she is a virgin. He locates the birthplace in or near Bethlehem, in an humble spot. Hence, he commands them to depart, first telling by what signs they will know her and search the world over for the maiden, bring her to him and he would kill her, They all disappear and Lucifer departs, when Mary appears in deep meditation.

"She is suddenly confronted by Michael, who announces to her her conception by the Holy Ghost. He tells her to fear naught, as he is her guardian angel, and she is the instrument of God. The shepherds come in singing songs of praise and exultation that the time approaches for the fulfillment of the prophesy in Isaiah, chapter 7. "Behold! A virgin shall conceive and bear a son, and shall call his name Emmanuel." At this juncture Lucifer returns followed by his imps, who communicate to him their inability to locate the maiden. They also inform him that the whole world is expecting the coming of the Messiah. They beg of him to give them her name to aid them in the search of her. At the pronunciation of her name, Michael appears upon the scene, reminds Lucifer of his former downfall, proclaims himself Mary's guardian angel, and advises Lucifer to desist from his evil intention, warning him of the consequences that will follow should he insist upon his evil course.

"After vigilant search Lucifer locates Joseph and Mary, and though through fear of Michael, he dare not injure the person of Mary, he poisons Joseph's mind against her, and Joseph becomes suspicious and jealous of his wife. Mary appears heavily grieved at Joseph's treatment of her, and recites that she finds no comfort day or night, and passes her time while Joseph is absent, in prayer and devotion.

"Night approaches and Joseph lies down to sleep, when he is awakened by an angel, who reassures him of Mary's faithfulness to him. He also makes known to Joseph the conception of Mary by the Holy Ghost. Joseph repentant, hastens to Mary's presence, falls upon his knees before her, implores her pardon for his treatment of her and reasures her of his love and confidence. The shepherds sing:

> "Lloren alla los demonios,
> Y lloren con afliccion,
> Que ya se abre misteriosa.
> El admirable encarnacion, etc

> "Let the imps of darkness weep,
> And may they weep with anguish,
> For there has been disclosed mysteriously
> The admirable incarnation.

"The shepherds pass out and Lucifer enters, furious at being again balked in his designs, giving vent to his rage. He is confronted by the angel Gabriel, whom Lucifer fails to recognize, but who shows by his conversation that he is an adversary who knows Lucifer's past and present history on earth, and he prophesies Lucifer's final defeat and his banishment:

> "Y asi no sabras, villano
> Que lo que el tiempo te advierte,
> Tu rabia sera la muerte,
> Y moriras triste sifano, etc.

> "And thus you shall not know, villian!
> What the times would warn you against.
> Your fury shall be your death,
> And you shall die sorrowfully, braggart!

"Gabriel vanishes and Lucifer calls up his imps,

with whom he holds counsel, and they plot the capture of Gabriel. They are surprised by Mary and Joseph who are on their journey to Bethlehem, and at sight of whom Lucifer and his confederates flee, saying;

> "Ya Maria sale del templo,
> Y Jose viene a su lado,
> Abra su boca el abismo,
> Sepulta a un desdichado, etc.

> "Already Mary leaves the temple,
> And Joseph is by her side.
> Open your mouth, Hell!
> And bury an unfortunate.

"Upon their arrival at Bethlehem, Mary and Joseph go from door to door, begging shelter for the night, while the shepherds are singing:

> "Un pobre hombre y una doncella,
> Que al lugar hemos venido,
> Abran nos de caridad,
> Den nos siquiera posada, etc.

> "A poor man and a maid
> Who to this place have come,
> Open to us for charity's sake,
> Give us at least a shelter.

"And they invariably received for reply:

> "Pues ninguno puede entrar,
> Porque no quiere mesonero,
> Solo que traiga dinero,
> Con que lo pueda pagar, etc.

> "No one can enter here,
> Because the innkeeper does not wish it,
> Unless you bring money,
> With which to pay for it, etc.

"At last they find shelter in the stable, and are glad to rest their weary feet, and the shepherds begin singing":

"Abranse las puertas,
Rompanse los velos,
Que viene a posear,
El rey de los cielos, etc.

"Open the doors,
Tear away the veil—
For there comes to seek shelter
The king of the heavens, etc.

"The scene now changes. Lying around a camp fire are shepherds, some asleep, others in low conversation. Suddenly one discovers a bright star in the East, which he joyfully announces to the others, when all in one voice, break out with hallelujahs and songs of praise."

"En el portal de Belen
Hay muy bella claridad,
Porqua ha nacido el Mesias
Y nos pondra en libertad.

Chorus: "Guerra y guerra le daremos,
Y guerra le hemos de dar
Al demonio y su infierno,
Ahora le haremos temblar,

"In the porch at Bethlehem
There is a beautiful illumination,
Because the Messiah was born there
And he will set us at liberty.

Chorus: "Battle upon battle we will give him,
And war again shall be given
To the devil and his infierno,
Now we will make him trouble.

"Two of the shepherds: Fevano and Parrado, continue singing and telling what beautiful presents of precious stones and jewels they will take as offerings to the church, until they are reminded by the gila (cook), to get their food ready, fill their knapsacks—as day is approaching and they must make an early start.

"Lucifer enters, filled with anguish and torment as he sees his power tottering. His emissaries have located the Christ child, and his plots and intrigues to entrap mother and child have proved fruitless, as they are constantly guarded by Michael and Gabriel. When still deliberating on what to do, shepherds approach on their way to Bethlehem, guided by the "star in the East." They are singing:

>"Al respaldo, hermanos mios,
>De un encumbrado cerro
>Pues dicen ya nacio
>El Redemtor de los cielos, etc.

>"Back, my dear brothers,
>Of a lofty hill
>They say there was born
>The Redeemer of heaven.

"Gila finishes the singing with the advice;

>"Pastores ya llega el dia
>En que alegres nos partamos
>Para el portal de Belen
>A ver un feliz milagro,
>Prevengan sus bastimentos,
>Dispongan muy bien sus jatos
>Para caminar alegres,
>Festejandonos con cantos.

>"Shepherds: the day has arrived
>On which we will gladly depart
>For the porch of Bethlehem
>To see a happy miracle.
>Prepare your lunches,
>Pack well your lunch baskets
>So as to travel pleasantly,
>Entertaining ourselves with songs.

"Lucifer hails them and in conversation advises them not to go to Bethlehem, as the road to it is dangerous, infested by beasts of prey, and covered with snow and ice, and says they have been deceived, as the Messiah had not yet come. They pay no heed to his advice, but continue their journey, selecting the best road for their sheep, which they take with them. As they near the mountains, a hermit comes out of a cave and joins them in their pilgrimage. He is old and bent, hair and beard are long and heavy, and he wears a long white tunic which is girdled with a thick white cord. From his neck hangs a rosary composed of white spools, to which is attached a crucifix, He is the clown of the company and with his merry jokes and jests keeps the shepherds in good humor on their tedious journey. They continue singing and must have covered quite a stretch before they come to the end of a song, the first verse of which is:

> "En risuenos cantos
> De los ruisenores
> Caminemos alegres
> Hermanos Pastores, etc.

> "In merry songs
> Of the nightingale
> Let us travel gladly
> Dear brother shepherds, etc.

"They stop on the road to take supper, and invite the hermit to partake of tortillas, cabrito (kid), pinole mesquite bean flour) and tamales (shuck dumplings.) Parrado leaves them while he goes to see the sheep. He returns and tells them that if each give him albricias (a present), he will tell them some wonderful news. After exacting a promise from each, he tells them that while out with the sheep, an angel appeared to him who said: "Gloria in excelsis, the Christ is come." Some tell him he has been dreaming, others that he is deceiving them and that they will not believe him. But at this juncture, Michael himself appears and confirms Parrado's story, and assures them of the birth of the Christ. He also warns them that Lucifer is again coming to confuse them, but that they must not be afraid of him, as he (Michael) will be with them. Lucifer arrives, asks for food and shelter because he is a stranger in a strange land. He further states that he is very rich and will divide his wealth with them. He and the hermit get into an altercation, and the hermit defends himself against Lucifer's attacks by merely holding up the crucifix in front of him. Lucifer is unsuccessful with the hermit, so he departs and visits the two shepherds, Bato and Cocharon, whom he tempts into partaking of a meal with him. These two are watching the sheep and hunger induces them to feast with the stranger, though they do not like his countenance. The other shepherds turn out to look for Bato and Cocharon, as the time for their coming into camp has past. They find the two very sick and bring them into camp, singing:

> Venid, Miguel, dichoso,
> Del lado cortesano,
> A sacar de prisiones
> A todo genero humano.

> Come, happy Michael,
> From that gentle side,
> To free from prison
> All mankind.

The shepherds have stopped to rest for the night, when an angel again appears, saying aloud: "Glory to God, the Christ is come." The hermit falls upon his knees in prayer while the shepherds join in songs of praise and thanksgiving.

Lucifer appears and is about to destroy them when Michael and his hosts appear, give him and his imps battle, vanquish him and put him in chains. Lucifer changes his tactics, and his repentance and promises seem so sincere that Michael's pity is aroused and he relents. He has the chains taken from Lucifer. Immediately Lucifer rallies his imps and begins combat against Michael and his hosts. Lucifer is again vanquished and is banished from earth forever. At this juncture Satan's tail is ignited and Lucifer and his host vanish amidst the noise made by the exploding firecrackers.

"The shepherds at last arrive at the manger, each one in turn praying before the image of Christ, and singing a verse in adoration; at the same time each presenting some offering, excepting Bartholomew, who is a ridiculously sleepy fellow and cannot shake off his drowsiness. Each one of the shepherds, even the cook, goes to him and pleads with him to get up and adore the Christ child; but he has some excuse for each one until at last patience ceases to be a virtue and two shepherds take him and deposit him in front of the altar. Either the fall, or the bright illumination falling upon him has the desired effect and he falls upon his knees in contrition and joins in the adoration. Two shepherds then come forward, take the streamers on either side of the cradle, and swinging the cradle to and fro, are joined by the others singing the Lullaby:

"Ah! que hermosura de nino!
Que boquita de coral!
Quieres que te tape
Con las telas de mi amor?
"O, quieres venirte a mi pecho?
Tu quieres que me arrime.
Al pesebre y te arrolle,
Al-or-or-or-or-or-or, etc.
"Ah! what beauty in a child!
What a little coral mouth.
Did you wish that I shall cover thee
With the weaving of my love?
"Or will you come to my breast?
You want me to approach
The crib and rock you?
Al-or-or-or-or-or-or.

"They then, each one in turn, kneel before the image, ask a blessing on Mary and Joseph, kiss the image and depart singing."

The Pastores were originally intended by the holy Friars to impress upon the minds of the rude untutored

Indians the truth of the principal mysteries of religion, but in the course of time, the religious drama passed through the unscrupulous hands of ignorant men and degenerated into a worldly show, now restricted to Mexican jacales or the opera house. This drama under the management of the old Friars was pure and dogmatic, but now, in order to render it more poignant, spicy and better adapted to worldly taste, new personages have been introduced, as for example, Gila (the Shepherds' Cook), a female, forsooth! as if these poor shepherds had the means to carry along with them a whole assortment of kitchen utensils. Then comes the grotesque and anachronistic hermit with his funny rosary made of spools. The substitution of St. Michael for St. Gabriel as the Archangel who announced to the Blessed Virgin Mary that she was to become the Mother of God, is also a grave scriptural error. When these objectionable innovations have been removed, the drama, as above described, deserves credit.

CHAPTER IV.

Cathedral of Puebla. The Venerable Palafox. Process of Cannonization Failed.

Before leaving Puebla let us pay a visit to the cathedral, the pearl of Mexican churches. It is not as large as the Cathedral of Mexico, being about 323 feet in length by 101 feet wide. By the richness of its decoration, distributed with faultless taste, it far surpasses all the large churches in America. It is almost impossible to give even a faint idea of the impression felt on first entering this beautiful building. Everything within it appears fresh and new. The corner stone was laid in 1532. Like all the cathedrals in this country, it stands apart in the midst of extensive grounds, and is located in the centre of the principal plaza, which is surrounded by a great number of angels standing on elaborate pillars. The most striking features of the exterior are the two massive towers flanking the main entrance. On one of these towers is an inscription declaring that it cost $100,000. In this tower there are eighteen bells, the largest of which weighs upwards of nine tons. With regard to the interior, it would be impossible to enter into details.

The whole work of ornamentation was carried out under the direction of a Mexican of Indian extraction. The sound judgment and excellent taste displayed in this work, as well as in many other works of art, are an evidence of the artistic instinct of the Mexican people. The high altar and onyx baldaquino above it, also the work of a Mexican, cost more than $300,000. This altar is composed of every variety of Mexican marble, the onyx peculiar to Puebla being used in the greatest proportion. The interior architecture is massive, but all heaviness disappears in the presence of its rich and bright decorations. There is not a square foot of wall or ceiling that is not covered with gilt carving, exquisite paintings, or high marble reliefs. Its sacristy, as large as an ordinary church, is in keeping with the cathedral, and contains the portraits of all the Bishops of Puebla who have governed that See for 360 years. Standing in the midst of such grandeur and treasures, all gladly donated for the glory of God by this Catholic people, who would think for a moment that Protestantism, with its soulless formalities, which are all it has to offer its neophytes, could ever hope to seduce the Mexican people from the Catholic faith?

Puebla is celebrated not only for its splendid cathedral, but also for the immense edifices which compose the Bishop's palace, the Major and Minor Seminaries for ecclesiastical students; the College of San Ildefonso, and the school for the Infantes (altar boys), attended by about one hundred bright intelligent boys. All these edifices are in the same block and are chiefly the work of the Venerable Palafox, formerly Bishop of Puebla and Viceroy of Mexico. Among the many eminent members of the Episcopate of ancient Mexico the name of Palafox stands conspicuous. The process of his beatification was introduced in Rome, but was set aside by the arguments of the Devil's Advocate. This requires a few explanations. The process of beatification is a long, laborious and expensive one. First, all the information which can possibly be procured, must be gathered regarding the life and actions of the candidate. This must be the sworn testimony of competent witnesses before the proper authorities. When we take into account the number of places in which a saint has been, and the number of persons who must be summoned from a distance, and then the writing out; the classifying, and the printing in huge folios of their accumulated evidence; we may form some idea of the trouble attending the very preliminaries of beatification. These ponderous tomes will not be admitted into the court unless there be petitions from Cardinals, Bishops, Generals of Order and various noteworthy persons for the institution of the suit, if we may so call it. Then there is the Devil's Advocate, a sharp learned theologian, whose business it is to cavil at every bit of evidence, and reject the facts if they be not sufficiently authenticated. Many a cause is stopped in its very beginning by this worthy gentleman. When the processes (such is the name given to the mass of evidence collected) have passed these scrutinies and leave is given for the introduction of the cause, the servant of God receives the title of Venerable. There are various questions to be discussed then: namely, whether religious worship has been offered or whether he has been called a saint. Any of these things would be a serious objection, and many causes stop here. His works are examined, and then there is a process regarding his sanctity in general. If these pass, the apostolic processes are formed. Then fifty years after the death of the Venerable, and not before, unless by dispensation, the examination of his every virtue is instituted. This may prove a failure; if so, the cause is finished. Three sessions are held upon this point of the question, and when it is carried, there is a decree published to the effect that the venerable servant of God did possess the theological and Cardinal virtues in a heroic degree. Then comes the discussion on the miracles. This is so severe that it has passed into a proverb that it is a miracle for a miracle to pass the sacred congregation.

Although the Venerable Palafox had practiced virtue in an eminent degree, worked miracles, written beautiful treatises on Christian perfection and on various other subjects, forming twenty folio volumes, the process of his beatification failed. Yet the monuments of his zeal; the Cathedral at Puebla, the numerous edifices erected by him for the education of youth, his numerous and pious treatises of devotion, history, and other branches of ecclesiastical lore will remain to proclaim him one of the greatest and most illustrious men who ever trod on Mexican soil.

Another monument of interest is the Jesuit's Church called "La Compania," which has a college attached. Twenty-one Jesuits are occupied in this College, where they teach all the branches of education besides a school of trades, comprising printing; watch making; typewriting; short hand; cabinet making; blacksmithing; mining, etc.

With regret we departed from Puebla, the cleanest city of Mexico, where tourists enjoy a sight not soon to be forgotten. How delightful to see in the early morning the snow-capped Popocatepetl gilt by the first rays of the rising sun!! Adios.

Not far from Puebla, a short distance from the road to Mexico, stands the town of Tlascala. There is seen the church of San Francisco, the foundations of which were laid in 1521, two years after the arrival of Cortez. Amongst the rich and historic relics in this church is preserved the pulpit from which the faith was first preached in the New World. Here also is the baptismal font where the four Tlascalan chiefs were baptized in the year 1520. All aboard! "Vamonos!" "Para Mejico?" "Si senor."

CHAPTER V.

City of Mexico. Arrival of the Monks. The Hand of God is There. Predictions. Protestantism a Failure. Don Pancracio.

"City of prodigies, hail! From thee irradiated the rays of faith." In order to understand the present state of religion and to be able to account for the multiplicity and splendor of the magnificent temples, convents and monasteries in Mexico: the work of over three centuries of Christianity and civilization, it is necessary to look for the causes which produced such wonderful results.

Paganism once reigned supreme in Mexico, but now the country is thoroughly Christian. We can only give a brief explanation of this fact. An object, which Cortez never lost sight of, was the conversion of the natives. It was Cortez who first requested that religious be sent from Spain. "I supplicate your Imperial Majesty," he says in one of his letters "that you would have the goodness to provide religious persons of good life and example for the conversion of the natives." And when the Franciscans arrived, it was in the following words that he presented them to the people of Mexico:

"These are men sent from God, and ardently desiring the salvation of your souls. They ask neither your gold nor your lands, for, despising all the goods of this world, they aspire only after those of the next."

In 1531, when there were only one hundred Franciscans and Dominicans in the whole country, the Auditors wrote to the Emperor, beseeching him to send out more monks, being doubtless of the same mind with a subsequent Viceroy of Mexico, who, when there was much question about building forts throughout the country, said that "towers with soldiers were dens of thieves, but that convents with monks were as good as walls and castles for keeping the Indians in subjection."

Quiroga filled with admiration of what the monks had already done, exclaimed: "I offer myself, with the assistance of God, to undertake the establishing of Christian communities similar to those of the primitive Church; for God is as powerful now as then, and I pray that this plan may be favored."

At the instance of Bishop Zumarraga, Queen Isabella sent out some pious women to instruct the young girls, but as they were not bound by vows, they soon married.

Up to the year 1600, more than 150 Franciscans had suffered martyrdom in the New World. "The blood of martyrs," said Tertulian, "is the seed of Christians."

Who does not see the hand of God in the conversion of Mexico! So marvelous was the conquest of Cortez, that he seems to have been an instrument in the hands of Providence for the accomplishment of its great designs with regard to Mexico. History contains nothing parallel with respect either to the boldness of the attempt or the success of its execution. The circumstances of these extraordinary transactions are authenticated by the most unquestionable evidence. Still they appear so wild and extravagent as to go beyond the bounds of fiction. Take for example the great battle of Otumba, which has no parallel in the annals of Rome or Greece. Prodigies of all kinds seem to indicate that the hour set by Divine Providence for the conversion of Mexico had arrived.

Supposed prophesies existed among the Aztecs regarding the coming of white men and friars into Mexico. We read in St. Anthony's Messenger that "the natives of Espanola are said to have received an oracle shortly before Columbus' arrival, announcing the coming of bearded men with sharp bright swords. The Yucatan records abound in predictions to the same effect, more or less clear. The most widely quoted is that of Chilam Balam, high Priest of Mani, and reputed a great prophet, who foretold that ere many years, there would come from the direction of the rising Sun a bearded white people, bearing aloft the cross, which he displayed to his listeners. Their gods would flee before the newcomers and leave them to rule the land; but no harm would fall on the peaceful who admitted the only true God. This Priest it was who erected the stone crosses found by the Spaniards, declaring them to be the true tree of the world. It is recorded that a Priest of Itsalan urged his people to worship the true God, whose word would soon come to them."

"Among the Mexicans," says Mendieta, "predictions were current, some four generations before the conquest, of the coming of bearded men, dressed in raiment of different colors, and with helmets on their heads. The idols would perish, leaving but one supreme God; war would cease; roads would be opened; intercourse established, and the husband would cherish but one wife."

The testimony is so abundant and explicit that many of these and other prodigies were at the time received, not only by Montezuma and his people, but by the neighboring nations, as the distinct announcement of the coming of the white, bearded men, who in truth appeared at the proper time in the person of the Spaniards.

Whatever may be thought of these forebodings, the fact stands, that for 360 years, the Mexicans have been and are Christians and Roman Catholics. They profess the true faith and are satisfied with it, for they know they are right. The broad seal of heaven is stamped on their faith. There is no room for doubt. This explains why Mexicans have adhered to the Catholic Church and no heresy has ever originated among them. This also explains why the several attempts of Protestant ministers in Mexico have always been a failure. Who has not heard of the Episcopal Bishop Riley? The American Protestant Bishops sent him to Mexico with a well filled purse. Since the promulgation of the "Leyes de reforma," there are excellent bargains to be had when one's conscience is not particularly tender on the subject of sacrilege. It appears that this Episcopal Bishop so comported himself as to fall under the censure of the American Bishops, who had sent him to Mexico; whereupon he defied their authority and set up a Mexican Episcopalian Church for himself. They protested against him, and he in turn protested against them in good Orthodox Protestant fashion. He refused to give an account of his administration. The church of San Francisco, one of the most beautiful in Mexico, having been confiscated by the government, was sold to Bishop Riley, but for some reason or other it was afterwards sold at auction, and Don Antonio Escandon became the owner of it. It is now under the control of the Archbishop of Mexico. The church has been reconsecrated and is now used by Catholics for divine service.

The Quakers, the Methodists, the Baptists, and

others have tried the experiment and failed. The Mexicans to become Protestants? No, never! Protestant missionaries may catch an occasional poor devil, but experience will teach that they have caught a tartar.

"Carramba!" exclaims Don Pancracio, "How many religions are imported to Mexico by the Yankees. We thought that Christ had instituted only one Church when He said 'My Church and not churches.' Now there come the thirteen different sects of Baptists, each of which says, 'we are the true church, and unless you are immersed neck deep in the river, you shall be damned.' 'No,' says the Quaker, 'baptism is not necessary at all.' We Mexicans, in our simplicity, prefer to believe Christ, who says: 'Unless a man be born again of water and the Holy Ghost, he cannot enter into the Kingdom of God.' By immersion? Carramba! How did St. Peter baptize his fellow-prisoners, when we know that the water he obtained by a miracle was scarcely sufficient to immerse a tom cat. Now there come the eight different sects of Methodists, fighting with each other on the dogmas of original sin and justification. The Presbyterians, old and new school, have no need of bishops, if they be predestinated. Episcopalians have bishops by the grace of Big Henry and Queen Bess, not by the grace of God and favor of the Holy See. The Universalists say 'that all shall be saved in the end;' then the eternal fire spoken of by Christ is a lie!! O Senores Protestantes! we do not hate you, but we hate and abhor your new-fangled doctrines; we are Christians, we are Catholics, go among the heathens, the Chinese and the Hindoos, who need Christianity. Why do you come to disturb us in the faith of our fathers? You say we are idolaters!!! Caramba, idolatras!!! when we Mexicans can say amen to the following curses, without incurring the displeasure of Mother Church:

"'Cursed is he that commits idolatry; and prays to images or relics and worships them.' Amen.

"'Cursed is he that believes the Virgin Mary to be more than a creature, that worships her or puts his trust in her more than in God.' Amen.

"You are welcome to work our mines, and get as much gold and silver as you can, but as to our faith, it is as impregnable as the fortress of Gibraltar."

Don Pancracio is rough in some of his expressions, but he gives the key-note of the situation of Mexico with regard to the religious question. A few hungry peons, or some ignorant upstarts may join one sect or another for the time being and for some temporal notions, but in time of trials and sickness you will see these poor prodigal sons come back to Mother Church.

The converts to Protestantism in Mexico as described to me by gentlemen of high standing in Church and State, consist of those who had never learned one page of the Chatechism. A few enterprising individuals, in the hope of a lucrative sinecure, join the Protestant business as they would a commercial firm, for there is money in it and very little to do. Is there one single instance of a Mexican becoming a Protestant in order to be a better Christian? Not one. Protestant preachers, besides disturbing the faith of a noble nation, put additional work on the Priests' shoulders when they are called upon at the hour of death to reconcile these stray sheep with the Church of God.

The mother of Melanchthon, at the hour of death, asked her son the following question: "My son, for the love of you I joined the new religion, now that I am going to appear before God, what do you advise me to do? "Mother," said he, "the new religion is the easiest to live in, but the Catholic religion is the best to die in."

If there are instances of Mexicans among the ignorant and lower class becoming Protestants, they are moved by temporal considerations only, like that poor man, who previous to joining a sect, went to the foot of the high altar, there to make a compromise with Almighty God. "Lord!" said he, I am going to leave you and tell you good-bye, but be not angry with me, for I promise to return as soon as times are better; those heretics over there promise me food and shelter for the children. Be patient, good Lord!" Or like that Mexican woman who had joined a sect for the same motives. The first time she went into the Protestant church the minister perceived a rosary in her hands and heard her saying the beads. "Oh, horror!" the minister exclaimed, "no idolatry, no superstition allowed here," and he snatched the rosary from her hands. "No se reza el rosario aqui? Adios, me voy:" "Is the rosary not recited here? Good-bye, I quit," said the woman, and she left after returning the money she had received that day.

No; Mexicans shall never become Protestants.

But the mill must be kept grinding out money, and more money is necessary for the spread of the gospel among the benighted Mexicans. A female missionary writing from Monterey, years ago, revealed the astounding fact that half of the population had been already converted to Protestantism, and if the brethren of the North would only send more material means, the whole population would soon be gained over to God and the pure gospel!!!

Agents and missionories of the sects may send to their Northern brethren glowing reports of the progress of the Gospel! how anxious the Mexicans are to hear the word of God and how eagerly they yearn for Protestant doctrine!! But, the real fact is, Mexicans are disgusted with the cold Protestant religious service. The reports forwarded from Mexico to the credulous brethren have been proven not only exaggerated but absolutely false, which explains the fact of the scarcity of material means sent to these pseudo-apostles of the Gospel.

When a fanatical pulpiteer has anything to say about Mexico, we may be sure that it is not possible for him to put down the bigotry that is in him. Mexico is a Catholic country, therefore there can be nothing good in it. That is his style of reasoning. Not long ago the chaplain of the Ohio penitentiary, a person named Winget, preached on Mexico to a congregation of convicts. His anti-Catholic prejudice was so marked that even the prisoners hissed him. This personage had visited Mexico and he told his hearers that "the degredation and superstition he witnessed there appalled him." He had much more to say in a similar strain, all to the effect that Mexican civilization was of the most degraded character. Fortunately for the cause of truth and justice a gentleman who took a trip through Mexico at the same time as Chaplain Winget also had something to say about what he saw in that country. This gentleman is General Brinkerhoff, President of the National Prison Congress and a member of the Ohio Board of State Charities. His statement is a complete refutation of the ministerial calumniator's assertions. For instance, this is what General Brinkerhoff, who is not a Catholic, has to say of the civilization of Mexico:

"Mexico was a revelation to me, as indeed, it was to the majority of our party. We labored under a wrong impression of the country, as do also the great bulk of the American people. What we found was surprisingly and interestingly unique and instructive. The conditions were entirely different from what we had expected, and the country as a whole, at no point what had been generally promised. It is due to the Catholic Church that Mexico has evolved from a chaos of savageness to one of the greatest nations of the globe. I am full of Mexico and her wonderful future, and I believe honestly that it is the one country for the man who has some modest capital and an unbridled energy." Preachers may rave and lie about Mexico, but honest men will make the truth known to the world, to the confusion of the calumniators.

CHAPTER VI.

Rambles through the city. Religious Aspect on the road to Toluca. Grand Scenery. The Passionists.

Here is the Plaza Mayor, a great rectangle 270 yards long by 200 yards in width, one side of which is occupied by the Cathedral, the grandest structure upon the continent of America. The National Palace, a huge, long building stands on the other side. Stone buildings of two or thee stories flank the plaza on the two remaining sides, The upper portion of these buildings are supported by massive pillars, forming arcades, and the ground floors in front are open. Through the colonnaded walks thus formed, called "Portales," crowds are continually streaming. One never tires of strolling about and watching the ceaseless movements and kaleidoscopic colors of the shifting mass of picturesque humanity. Now and then we notice a native woman with the Astec features. Again, come the peddlers carrying around trays of dulces, cakes and fruits, such as chirimoya, or angels' food, the most luscious fruit of Mexico; and the zapote, of which there is a great variety. Strawberries are sold the whole year round. Passing through the beautiful streets of Plateros and San Francisco we visit the Church of "La Profesa," the most beautiful of the city. Thence we pass to the street of Cadena where the Presidential Mansion stands. It was my good fortune to pay a visit to Dona Carmelita, the President's wife, who kindly and considerably helped me to carry out the object of my visit to the city of Mexico. The "Alameda," the "Paseo de la Reforma," the castle of Chapultepec, the historical Molino del Rey, Churubusco, and Contreras are favorite resorts for tourists.

Excepting the Freemasons—a pernicious sect, dangerous to Church and State, the military and civil officials —with a few honorable exceptions—and the clique of upstarts, both young and old, who pretend to know all "de omni re scibili et de quibusdam aliis" and relegate the science of salvation and the knowledge of God among women— Mexico is a religious city.

Every Sunday the 200 churches are crowded during Masses, which are celebrated for the convenience of the greater number, and even the 12 o'clock Masses for the benefit of stragglers and sluggards are well attended. Even on week days I have seen churches crowded with devout Christians, and from twenty to fifty approaching the Holy Table. Truly, the city of Mexico is a city of churches; chapels, and of sincerely devout Christians.

Our Lady's feasts in Mexico are especially splendid. Besides the Church devotions, the people further honor their sweet Mother by decorating their balconies with draperies of silk, embroidered in silver threads. Even in the poorer streets one may see a bit of calico and a strip of cheap lace, hanging from many a humble balcony. Every church, even the poorest, is then radiant with decorations and redolent with flowers. In the wealthier edifices, blue and white silk or satin, intersperced with silver or gold, is draped about the altars, the pillars, and the pulpit; and choice flowers and plants peep out between gorgeous jeweled candelabra and myriads of gleaming tapers. Add to this, a mass of kneeling, supplicating people; grand orchestral music and the deep resonant voices of a male choir; a more heavenly scene can scarcely be imagined: these feasts resemble a beautiful dream of heavenly visions. Adios!

In the early morning we left the city of Mexico. The atmosphere hung heavy over our heads, clouds hid the sky, the valley was impregnated with the mephitic exhalations of the night. The "Vamonos!" with its peculiar accent from American lips unused to the sweet Castilian, announced that the iron steed was in readiness. "Vamonos." "Si Senor, cuando guste," answers a mocking bird close by, but one without feathers. The valley of Mexico is soon passed and we enter the upgrade with the assistance of an additional engine. The twenty-three bridges, built over the meandering and rapid stream running through wood and dale, reveal a magnificent work of engineering. The surrounding scenery enraptures the soul, and makes us look from nature to nature's God. Meditation becomes natural. "God is admirable in His works?" As we ascend, the sky grows clearer and the atmosphere cooler. Our engines appear exhausted when we reach "Las Cruces," the highest point. The down grade opened to our view one of the grandest scenes I ever enjoyed. As our train emerged from a dense thicket, lo! on our left, 1200 feet below, an immense plain stretched out through a varying panorama of wonderful and enchanting scenes. Scattered about the verdant plain below are seen villages with churches, steeples, and domes, numerous haciendas and ranchos extending far beyond our view. In front of us, a few miles south of the city, stands the majestic, snow-capped "Nevada de Toluca," which is an extinct volcano 15,000 feet high. It is said that on a clear day, both the Pacific Ocean and the Gulf of Mexico may be distinguished from its summit!!!

Toluca is well built and its climate cool and salubrious. At the time of the Conquest it was an important Aztec pueblo and tradition assigns its foundation to the Toltecs.

There are several beautiful churches in the city, all built by the old Franciscan Friars. In the heart of the city may be seen enormous pedestals and foundations filled with huge blocks. What are they? A certain man with ideas broader than his exchequer, conceived the idea of reproducing the Cathedral of Mexico, adopting the same style of architecture and exactly the same dimensions as that unique ecclesiastical edifice of the New World; but as there was no King of Spain to back him, his undertaking was a failure, notwithstanding that he was an extraordinary man and a genius. But sometimes there appears something nobly wild and extravagant in great natural geniuses.

There are two religious communities of Priests here; the one is composed of Passionists, who occupy a beautiful monastery built on a tract of sixty acres, the gift of two sisters of the City of Mexico, who donated at the same time, $50,000 for the erection of a fine Gothic church. The place is called "El Ranchito," and is situated on the outskirts of the city. The Fathers call it "The Retreat," because it is a place where men gather for a week to meditate on the "eternal years." From my room in the monastery I could see, every morning, Indians, men and women, carrying on their shoulders heavy burdens of wild fruits which they had gathered on the side of the "Nevada." I was greatly edified to see those simple souls enter the house of God, there to perform their morning devotions before carrying to the market the fruits which they had gathered from the field of God. The second community is composed of thirteen Priests from Spain. These two religious houses enjoy perfect liberty and are unmolested, notwithstand ing the tyranical "Leyes de Reforma." There exists in this city, the capital of the State of Mexico, strong evidences of a vigorous Catholic faith!

I visited a wealthy gentleman, a cripple, who invited me to enter the next room, where the Blessed Sacrament was kept; he had obtained that special privilege from Pope Pius IX, on the condition that a Chaplain be attached to that domestic sanctuary to say Mass once a week. There exists in the Mexican Republic a great number of domestic chapels, sumptuously adorned, some few enjoying the same privilege as the one just referred to.

CHAPTER VII.

Morelia. A Remarkable Episode. Pazcuaro. Indian Work of Art. A Famous Picture. The River Lerma. Lake Chapala. A Fish Story.

Leaving Toluca we took the branch road at Acambaro. At the start we entered a very circuitous up grade, now seeing the city at the left, then at the right, which caused a lady traveler to exclaim: "Oh! how many villages around here." Morelia is one of the most beautiful and romantic cities of the Republic. Here, it is said, are found the most remarkable specimens of beauty, both male and female. But as I am no judge of beauty, I leave the question to the court of Aesthetics.

It was my good fortune to take up my lodging with a Monsignor, canon of the Cathedral, to whom I had a letter of recommendation. I spent twelve days very agreeably with him. I transcribe the following facts, known by all the inhabitants of the city, exactly as I received them from the lips of the Monsignor himself.

Shortly after his election as Canon of the Cathedral of Morelia, Father Velez had the misfortune of being totally deprived of his sight. He remained blind nine years. One day, at 9 o'clock, just before retiring to rest, he knelt on his prie-Dieu and offered the following prayer and vow to Our Lady of Guadalupe: "Oh my Heavenly Queen and Mother! it is now exactly nine years since this affliction fell upon me. I always submitted to the infliction sent me by your Divine Son, but oh! Mother, how I wish to be able to render some services to the Church of your Son! I am strong and my pecuniary means are abundant! Oh Mother dear! if you obtain from your Son the return of my sight, I promise and vow to use all my fortune for the education of the orphans and the poor girls of the city, and furthermore I will make use of my restored sight only for the glory of God!" After this the holy man retired to his couch. The following morning he went to his lavatory, washed his face, and behold! he saw! He fell on his knees, gave thanks to Jesus and Mary, and ran to the Bishop's palace without his customary attendant. "Bishop," he said: "I see your Lordship, and I came alone; my sight is as perfect as it was ten years ago." He then related to his Lordship all the circumstances of his marvelous cure, and when he asked all faculties to carry out the object of his vow, the Bishop answered him: "Nothing can be refused to one so well privileged by Heaven." Now, there stands in the middle of the city, the grand institution of Our Lady of Guadalupe, with its hundred orphans and 2,500 girls, who receive a gratuitous education imparted by seventy female teachers, all expenses being borne by this prodigious benefactor; and I am able to certify that during the few days it was my pleasure to be his guest, I never saw him raise his eyes whilst walking in the streets or visiting his institution. Such a modest and unassuming man I never met in my life.

Twenty-two miles from Morelia is Pazcuaro, built on an eminence surrounded by hills from which is seen the most picturesque lake in Mexico, much resembling the famous lake of Gerarmer in the mountains of the Vosges in Lorraine, but much larger. A steamboat is continually plying on its limpid waters for the pleasure of tourists.

On one side of the lake there was formerly a city of 50,000 Indians, and it was an episcopal see, but it is now an insignificant village, remarkable only for its numerous ruins.

In the sacristy of the Church of San Francisco at Pazcuaro where the Priests vest for Mass, there is a large table of peculiar workmanship. It is the work of a poor Indian and a sort of mosaic, composed of seventy kinds of wood. There are birds, crosses, chalices, angels, and many other beautiful designs inlaid in its surface. The Indian worked eighteen years at it. He undertook this tedious task as a labor of love in thanksgiving for his conversion to Christianity. This masterpiece is valued at $85,000.

At Celaya in the Church of "El Carmen," there exists a picture which has attracted the attention of both American and English notabilities. It is a large painting by a Mexican artist, representing the Immaculate Conception. The Blessed Virgin stands majestically on a brilliant chariot, surrounded by a multitude of angels and supported by the four great doctors of the Church, Saints Gregory, Augustine, Jerome, and Leo; under the four wheels of the chariot are seen the grim faces of the four arch-heretics Arius, Nestorius, Luther, and Calvin, who are being crushed by the huge vehicle. The parish Priest, Rev. Father Gongora, told me that an American gentleman had offered him $20,000 for the picture. "My predecessor," said the Priest, "refused £20,000 sterling, which was offered by an English Lord for the same picture. That masterpiece shall not leave my church as long as I live," Celaya possesses four magnificent parochial schools built by a pious and rich lady, who also pays the teachers' salaries. These schools are admirably equipped.

On the way to Guadalajara, at a short distance from the railroad are three points of the highest interest to travelers who visit them for the first time. The lovely valley of the Lerma, recalled to my memory some of the scenes which had been the delight of my younger days in the valleys of the Moselle and Meuse in Lorraine. The Lerma river, which cuts its way from a plateau to a lower level, forms an enormous cañon, the perpendicular sides of which are two thousand feet high. At the top of the chasm, you are in a temperate climate; but at the bottom you get a taste of the torrid temperature which must be felt to be appreciated. Here the vegetation is vigorous, and nearly all the tropical fruits such as the banana, orange, mamey, chirimoya and zapote, abound on every side. This place is called the "Barranca."

The next place of interest is the falls of Juanacatlan, which resemble the Niagara Falls. They are really a miniature of that mighty cataract. There is the horse shoe, the island on the brink of the precipice; the rapids above and below, and the awful roar as at Niagara. The Lerma seems to be trying to pour all the waters of Lake Chapala over the falls at once. The river here is 560 feet wide, and falls sixty-five feet. The Chapala Lake, the largest in Mexico 1,300 square miles, is very interesting. A small steamer makes the tour of the lake daily. The depth of the lake has never been ascertained and it is filled with fish. The small fry especially are delicious, A basket containing 100 fried fish with a few tortillas thrown in, may be bought at the stations for 50 cts. As we were enjoying the contents of such a basket, one of the travelers, an old Frenchman, related the following fish story:

"Voltaire and Piron were enemies. One day the literati of Paris were invited to a social feast. Voltaire had said, 'If that rascal Piron is there I will not go, unless he gives his word of honor that during the meal he will say only four words.' Piron consented. The two enemies were seated at the same table opposite to one another, the one loquacious, and the other as mute as a post. A large dish of small fried fish was put on the table, Voltaire remarked: 'Of these fish I can eat as many as Samson killed of the Philistines.' 'With the same jaw!' added Piron. There went the four promised words agreed upon. The next day, Piron called on Voltaire, rang the bell, but as no answer came he withdrew, after writing in large letters the word 'rascal' on a dusty desk close by. A few days after the two men met on the street. 'I called on you the other day,' said Piron. 'Yes,' answered Voltaire, 'I saw your visiting card on the desk!'"

Hoping I shall be forgiven for this digression, I return to my subject.

CHAPTER VIII.

Guadalajara. Leon. A great painting. Guanjuato. Our burros. The Valenciana mine. Zacatecas.

The beautiful city Guadalajara the Florence of Mexico, lies in the valley of the Lerma. It is the second city of Mexico in population, and was founded in 1542. It is justly called the Athens of Mexico. Many Bishops, occupying Episcopal Sees in the Republic, as well as eminent lawyers and doctors hail from Guadalajara.

North of the Plaza de Armas is the Cathedral, a noble edifice with a rich facade, twin towers, and a beautiful dome.

The manufacturing interests of Guadalajara are important, and every stranger is interested in its pottery which has attained a world-wide fame, being the finest in Mexico. In almost every city or village in Mexico, pottery of some sort may be obtained, but the beautiful article turned out at Guadalajara excites the envy of every other place and commands the admiration of every person who sees or uses it. Water kept for half an hour in a Guadalajara jug, is almost as cool as ice water. About four miles from the city is the picturesque village of San Pedro, on an elevation from which may be obtained a magnificent view of the city below and the surroundings.

In my visits to clergymen in the city, as well as in Morelia, Mexico City, Puebla, and Leon, I was agreeably surprised to find immense libraries ranging from two to ten thousand volumes, treating on Pathology, Theology, Civil and Canon Law, Science, Aesthetics &c. The clergy as a class are generally highly educated and learned. In my first audience with archbishop Lopez, I was singularly struck by his personal appearance. His Grace reminded me at once of Pope Leo; the resemblance is striking; the same age, the same stature and noble bearing.

After a thirteen days' sojourn in Guadalajara, where I was the happy guest of a compatriot of mine from Lorraine, the manager of the splendid hotel "Humboldt," I started for Leon. This city which once was the second of the Republic, but is now the fourth in population, has many points of interest. The Calzada or Paseo, about a mile from the main plaza, is finely shaded by a triple avenue flanked by rich fields and gardens. The gardens of many of the poor residents in the outskirts of the city are fenced by rows of the "Organos" or tree cactus, which presents as impenetrable a barrier as a barbed-wire fence.

The manufacturers of Leon are principally leather and leather goods. Another industry is the weaving of the blue rebozos, or shawls, which are everywhere worn by the women of Mexico.

It is stated that Léon is the most religious city of the Republic. The place is styled "the city of refuge."

There is in the Cathedral of Leon a beautiful picture representing the Queen of Heaven, the origin of which was related to me as follows: "A venerable Jesuit, Father John Anthony Genoveci, a man of great piety and zeal for the salvation of souls, lived at Palermo, Sicily, where he was considered a Saint. There also lived in the same city a pious woman, who was by her prayers, a great help to the Jesuit missionary. These two holy personages worked wonders of conversions. One day in the year 1722, the Blessed Virgin appeared to the woman and commanded her to have an image of her, the Queen of Heaven, painted on canvas. The woman obeyed and forthwith started for the studio of a celebrated painter of Palermo who went to work and produced the picture according to the directions given him by the woman. This picture did not please the Blessed Virgin who appeared a second time, and ordered another to be painted. The second picture was also rejected. A third attempt was made by the same artist according to the minutest details given to the pious woman by the Queen of Heaven herself. This third picture received the approbation of Mary, who seeing it smiled benignly and bleesed it with her own hand. Father Genoveci carried this sacred painting in all his missions and wrought wonderful conversions for the space of ten years throughout the Kingdom of Sicily.

On the 2nd of July, 1732, this same painting was placed in the Jesuit church called 'La Compania' which is now the Cathedral of Leon, Mexico. It was sent by Father Genoveci himself from Sicily. On the reverse of the painting is the following inscription: "This picture is the original which came from Sicily and was blessed by the Holy Virgin herself." Signed by the Jesuit Fathers Joseph Mary Genoveci, Joseph Mary Monaco, Joseph Xavier Alagua, and Francisco Bonilla.

The picture's invocation is "Our Holy Mother of the Light," and it is universally known that since the advent of the holy likeness, Leon has been exempt from epidemics, or any other public calamity. It may justly be called "The City of Mary."

Guanajuato is certainly the quaintest city of the Mexican Republic. It was founded by the Spaniards in 1554, and occupies a narrow ravine upon each side of which are high, rocky cliffs. No city in Mexico is more picturesque. Entering at Marfil, the rocky ravine, the bottom of which barely affords room for the road, and the little Rio Guanajuato, which has been walled in to save every inch of space, the visitor passes between tier after tier of adobe or stone houses which seem to have grown out of the earth itself, or, as an old Spaniard told me: "Guanajuato was built in the sky, and the houses were let fall pell-mell."

One morning we hired two burros and went up to the Valenciana mine, the richest ore vein in Mexico. After one hour's assent through cliffs over a circuitous rocky road, we reached the summit, from which we had a full view of the city below.

We visited the superintendent of the mine, a special friend of my companion, a Priest of the city. We were offered the privilege of being let down in a large bucket, and visiting the subterranean city, in which there are over seventy streets, all bearing the names of Saints; we respectfully declined the kind offer, awed by the immense depth. We were satisfied with an inspection of the plan of the mine. It is simply wonderful.

The village close by, inhabited by 5,000 miners, possesses a church built by the owners of the mine. It is of immense dimensions, of a correct Moorish style of architecture, and cost over one million dollars.

In the large yard of the mine we saw 300 women and girls, each provided with a hammer and a basket, separating the richest ores from the poorest. Their salary is twelve and a half cents a day, some get as much as eighteen, and a few, being experts, are paid the large amount of twenty-five cents!! Upon my asking them how they could live on such scanty pay, they answered: "Senor, one cent's worth of coffee, one cent's worth of sugar, and one cent's worth of tortillas for breakfast, the same for dinner and the same for supper; thus we save three cents and a half every day." Still these people are happy and strikes are unknown among them!!

After having accepted a few specimens of the richest ores from the superintendent, we bestrode our jaded burros, and the descent of the mountain was more harrassing to us than its ascent.

Zacatecas is a very interesting place, full of strange sights. Away up upon the mountain called "La Bufa" is the shrine which the Mexicans love to visit, some of them even scaling its steep sides upon their hands and knees as an exceptional penance which they have imposed upon themselves, in order to obtain some special favors. Guadalupe, some six miles distant, is reached by a tramway. The cars, operated by the "gravitation system," start slowly, but soon whirl down the steep hills, pass by the queer adobe houses, now crossing over a bridge, then dart through a gulch around some huge boulders, or by the yawning mouth of some mine. In this city of Guadalupe is seen the convent from which the Franciscan Friars departed who together with their brethren of Queretero, evangelized Texas.

CHAPTER IX.

Back to the City of Mexico. Tula. At the Station; *Maguey Tostado*, Marquez; *Pulque*, *Guayavas*. Queretero; *Opals*. Celaya; *Cajetas*. Irapuato; *Fresas*. Aguas Calientes; *Frutas*. Chihuahua; *Leche*. Arizona, California.

Returning to the city of Mexico on business concerning the object of my tour through this romantic and picturesque country, I took a train of the Mexican Central en route for Paso del Norte. Before leaving this land of wonders, it may be of interest to transcribe here a few of the notes from my memorandum book.

The first place of interest on this road is the "Tajo de Notchistongo," a great canal commenced in 1607 for the purpose of draining the valley of Mexico. A fine view of this remarkable work may be had from the train. Tula, the next station, is one of the oldest towns of the country; it is called "the Ancient of days." It is noted for its Toltec ruins and relics. Here the Indian vendors run around the train crying out "Maguey tostado!" "Pulque!" very refreshing and medicinal.

The next place of any importance is San Juan del Rio, a very pleasing little town of 18,000 inhabitants. From here the train in climbing the sides of the mountains gives the passengers a fine view of the beautiful valley below, and at Marquez station reaches the highest point of the line 8,000 feet above sea level. Barley and other cereals, I saw harvested in February. Preserves of "Guyavas" are the specialties sold at the station. For fully an hour the train passes through orchards covered with fruit trees in great variety. The celebrated haciendo and factories of Hercules are now reached, and in a few minutes Queretero, an old city dating back to the Aztecs in 1445, comes in view. Here we behold a grand stone aqueduct four miles long and in many places supported by lofty arches often reaching to a hundred feet in height; it is a marvel of skillful and substantial work and brings pure water to the city. A small stream flows through the town furnishing irrigation, all that is needed in this whole land to make it prolific in grain and fruit.

At the station opals and a great variety of fruit are sold for a trifle. Celaya, a station two miles from the city is noted for the manufacture of "Cajetas." As soon as the train arrives, a crowd of men, women and children beseige the passengers, crying out in all the notes of the scale, "Cajetas de Celaya." This delicious food is composed of milk and other ingredients put up in wooden boxes and sold for twenty cents.

The next place of importance is Irapuato, the paradise of strawberries, which grow in immense fields under the gentle rays of a semi-tropical sun and are nourished by irrigation. They are offered for sale at the railway station every day in the year, and there is no hour of day or night when a passenger train reaches this point that the cry of "fresas" is not heard. When you buy a basket of strawberries at this station, look out or else you may find more straw than berries in the basket.

At Aguas Calientes the passengers are offered beautiful flowers and a great variety of tropical and semi-tropical fruits. Beautiful drawn work is brought to all trains by the vendors and sold at very low prices.

Chihuahua station offers the passengers the best milk and honey in the country, owing to the surrounding hills being covered with thyme and other odoriferous plants and flowers.

Farewell, land of sunshine and flowers!

We crossed the Rio Grande at Paso del Norte and trod again on Texas soil after a six months' absence. El Paso, Texas is comparatively a new place. Once I heard the late Col. John Ford relate that in early days he, accompanied by another American gentleman and some Indians, had opened the first road from San Antonio to El Paso. At that time El Paso consisted of one family who cultivated a cornfield on the bank of the river.

Passing in front of Fort Bliss, the train took us to Tucson, Arizona, where I was the guest of Bishop Bourgade. During my sojourn there I visited the celebrated mission and church of San Xavier del Bac, distant from Tucson about ten miles. The church is a large and beautiful building of Byzantine architecture, with rich interior, ornamental paintings and bas-reliefs around the principal altars. There are more than forty statues in niches on each side of the altar. The village is divided between two tribes of Indians of different nations. Mass is celebrated there every Sunday and Thursday by a Priest from Tucson. The soil of Arizona is covered with monuments of the Franciscan missions and the blood of martyrs there also became the seed from which sprang the conversion of many thousand Indians.

California, at present so renowned on account of rich gold mines, was no less remarkable for its Franciscan missions, and the name of the great patriarch is inseperably joined to the Queen City of the Pacific—San Francisco. The missions of Upper California were founded exclusively by the Franciscans, and the traveler who, from Los Angeles to San Francisco, visits the twelve or more half-ruined monuments, which were erected by the zeal of the sons of St. Francis, cannot help exclaiming; "the hand of God was there;" and 75,000 converted Indians are the proof of the assertion.

The hand of man passed there also and destroyed the work of the holy friars. Some of the missions are partly restored, especially those of Santa Barbara and San Gabriel, the former being now occupied by a community of Franciscans whose Prior was assassinated by a crank a few years ago. Now let us visit the ancient city of the Southwest.

CHAPTER X.

Santa Fe. Archbishop Lamy. To Europe. Ditched. Niagara Falls. Across the Ocean. Brest. Terrific tempest. Grande Chartreuse.

Santa Fe is without doubt the oldest city in America, having been occupied in 1550 by the Spaniards and before that by the Indians: but when it was built, no one can tell.

The Governor's palace, the Church of San Miguel, an old dwelling under the shadow of the church, and the church of "El Santo Rosario" are the most precious relics of the past. San Miguel church, which I could see from the room I occupied in the College of the Christian Brothers, has withstood the storms of more than 300 years. The Governor's palace is nearly as old. It is a one-story adobe building with inner partitions five or six feet thick, a portal in front and a "tout ensemble" which it is impossible to reconcile with the commonly accepted idea of a palace.

In 1692, Don Diego Vargas of Spain, with a force of 300 men, was sent to conquer New Spain, of which Santa Fe was the most important city.

Borne upon the back of a mule in the midst of his army, was an image of the Virgin Mary which Vargas had brought from Spain. Outside the city an altar was built; the image was placed upon it and here Vargas knelt while he besought the Virgin's help in the forthcoming battle, vowing that if she should grant him success, he would at once erect a church in her honor. The contest soon followed, and against great odds he came off victorious after a terrible struggle lasting eleven hours. The church was erected at once. This edifice was called "El Santo Rosario," and it still stands, a well-preserved old adobe in which services are frequently held.

During my sojourn in this city of ancient memories, in 1887, Archbishop Lamy related to me many thrilling episodes too numerous to be described here. The Spanish and Mexican Priests whom he found on his arrival in his newly erected diocese had hitherto been under the jurisdiction of the Bishop of Durango, and with reluctance accepted the new Bishop's authority. Upon this, Bishop Lamy undertook a long and tedious trip to Durango on horseback to settle the difficulties with the Mexican Bishop.

About this time I was preparing to go to Rome as a Delegate to the General Chapter of our Order. The greatest and most lasting impression I experienced during my trip to New York, from which port I should sail, was the following: At 4 o'clock a. m. we were suddenly awakened from our sleep and the next moment we found ourselves in a ditch with the whole train, composed of seven coaches and freight cars. No one was very seriously injured. My skinless elbows and knees required a two months' dressing to heal. One mile from the wreck was a farmer's house, where we took our breakfast at 10, consisting of bacon, biscuits and coffee. At 6 o'clock p. m. we were on board a new train.

The superstitious class among the passengers attributed the wreck to the presence of a Catholic Priest; but four rotten ties and the softness of the road-bed occasioned by heavy rains, were the real cause of the derailment.

We now reach Niagara Falls. Sublime! Silence! this wonder is beyond description. Among the latest calamities the following evoked tears from my eyes. A lady from England with her three little children, two girls and a boy, were standing upon the bridge which leads from the American side to Goat Island. They were admiring the foaming water as it rushed forward to the brink of the American falls for its final leap into the vast chasm below. Suddenly the boy lifted his little sister, about 6 years of age, and held her over the railing of the bridge, and said to her, "I am going to throw you into the water." This was done in boyish sport, but it had a fatal result. The little darling was seized with fright, gave one piercing scream, made one violent effort to grasp the railing. This caused her brother to lose his hold of her. There was a splash, the mother sank in a faint upon the bridge, uttering as she fell: "My God! my child, my darling child!" With one bound the boy cleared the railing and plunged into the seething waters in the vain effort to save his sister, but the cruel water swept both with lightning speed over its awful brink: two little lives were lost, and a mother's heart was broken. Those who were present will never forget that poor mother's heartrending cries, as she passed from her faint, exclaiming in the supreme agony of grief: "My children, my darling children! Oh! where are my darling children!"

My first voyage across the ocean had nothing worthy of note. Our cabin passengers numbered sixty-three. The Brest light-house came in sight after breakfast. There emerged from the steerage a young Frenchman in an advanced stage of consumption, a mere skeleton, with just $2 in his purse. He was going to Pau, in the south of France, there to die among his own. We raised $45 among the passengers to enable him to reach his destination.

On reaching Brest, my fellow travelers, all Americans, asked me to look for the best hotel, and to order a dinner, table d'hote. I made the bargain for 300 francs. When my friends heard of the price, they looked disappointed. "What kind of a dinner are we going to get for one dollar a piece? We want a real good, genuine table d'hote, French style." "Gentlemen," I said, "the bargain is made, the maitre de cuisine is already at work with his aides." After the dinner, which consisted of three courses, with two kinds of wine at our discretion and a splendid desert, all my companions were highly pleased and told the landlord: "Nous reviendrons." (We will come back and patronize you again.)

On my way to Paris, I had with me in the same compartment of the train two young Frenchmen, who began to converse in broken English on topics rather irreligious and sometimes tresspassing on the limits of common decency. "Young gentlemen," I said, "your conversation is disagreeable to me."

"Oh, we did not expect you would understand us."

"Well, my young fellows, your conversation is just as bad in English as it would be in French; desist, or else I will report you at the next station." They became as mild as lambs.

On my return trip across the Atlantic, in the month of November, we experienced such a tremendous tempest, that for three days we were in imminent danger. On the third day we were so furiously tossed to and fro that I was deprived of all control over my movements. I tried to go on deck, but the sailors opposed my progress. The huge waves rushed by at a furious pace; great seas rolled into the ship at the bow and filled the air with spray. The wind rose higher and higher; it roared louder and louder; then came the hurricane; the sailors clad in shapeless garments of oil cloth, ran with extreme difficulty to and fro, the boatswain's whistle or his loud voice directing their movements; all portended a disaster. Rev. Father Montillot, a Jesuit and fellow passenger, who is now stationed at the College of Grand Coteau, Louisiana, came to me and exclaimed: "Father, we are doomed; this is our last day; let us prepare and be in readiness to render to the passengers all the spiritual assistance we can." At once, with great difficulty, I went on deck, and casting a miraculous medal into the sea, I exclaimed: "Oh Mother, appease the waves." Then crawling on my knees, I reached the windlass at the prow, where I pinned another medal, saying: "Oh! Mother, guide our ship." A sailor seeing me, exclaimed in a distressing tone of voice: "Malheureux, que faites-vous la? (Unhappy man, what are you doing there?) A jerk of the ship may throw you into the sea." I went down to my berth. The next day all danger was over. How I sighed for solid ground! Oh! give me the plains of Texas!! The plains of the Atlantic are too treacherous.

Yet, after many years I undertook a fourth voyage across the sea. The General Chapter of the Congregation of the Oblates was to take place in Rome, and I was invited to the solemn assembly. The thought of Lourdes, Loretto and Rome at once dissipated the terrors of the ocean. To see Rome and die was one of my greatest aspirations.

Cheerful I started. This time the sea was perfectly calm. Nearly everyone was on deck, and we were thrown very much together. In fact, we got thoroughly into the fraternizing spirit, and all the passengers were on the most familiar terms. One day the wind fell to our stern. All the sails were hoisted and the vessel looked very important in her full dress, and we advanced very rapidly during the night. The next day after breakfast, I happened to remark, "At noon the bulletin will show over 400 miles." Immediately twenty-four passengers came forward to bet against me. I invested. A pool of $25 was made. The understanding was as follows: If the number of miles be above 400, the pool falls to the priest. Chances were taken by my twenty-four opponents, ranging from 377 to 400. At noon the bulletin marked 412 miles in the last twenty-four hours. The pool was mine. The rest of the trip was equally pleasant till we landed at Brest.

After a few days of rest I chose some of the most remarkable points of interest to visit, and chief among them was "La Grande Chartreuse." I shall merely notice the interior life and mortifications of the monks at the Grand Chartreuse. The Carthusians are the only religious who are never allowed to eat meat. They have a great monastic fast, which lasts from the 14th of September to Easter; and during that time, with few exceptions, they have only one meal a day. They are frequently interrupted in their sleep. The night service begins at 12 and lasts till 2. The dress of the Fathers is entirely of white wool. The use of linen is forbidden. Even their sheets are of wool. The Carthusians are a living example of the fact that asceticism is not injurious to health, for they reach a great age. I have seen several who looked to be over 80. The world may say: "They are murderers; they commit suicide." The fact of longevity contradicts this erroneous idea. Excess in eating and drinking kills more human beings than wars and epidemics ever did.

One of the Popes offered to relax the rule of abstinence and fasting. The Carthusians sent a protest, a deputation of twenty-seven of their number, the youngest of whom was 80, while the others varied between 90, 93 and 95. Such an appeal was more eloquent than words, and the Pope was convinced. Abstinence and fasting are the best physicians. Who does not know the story of Cornaro, a celebrated Italian physician? At 40, fast living had reduced him to the appearance of a skeleton. His friends had lost all hope. Cornaro began a new life and a new diet consisting exclusively of vegetables, fruit, and a glass of good old wine. He died at the age of 99 years.

CHAPTER XI.

Lourdes. Fr. Domenech. Cardinal Langenieux. She was cured. Power of Mary. Protestant Lady Cured and Converted. Marseilles.

Hail! rocks of Massabielle. The instant you reach the hallowed spot you feel at once the touch of the supernatural. I shall simply relate my impressions.

The first impression on my arrival at Lourdes, was produced by the sight of afflicted and praying pilgrims. The general spectacle was one of suffering invalids who, unable to obtain alleviation from natural agents, had come to ask their deliverance from a supernatural one. Directing my steps to the scene of the apparition, I entered the grotto and saw stacks of crutches, canes and mechanical appliances of every kind and shape for the relief of lameness and distorted limbs; ex-votos by the hundred; all presenting vivid evidences of the most wonderful cures. Then there is the spring which had issued forth under the hand of Bernadette in obedience to the Blessed Virgin.

A short distance from the grotto is a marble slab, on which I knelt and prayed. It bears the following inscription: "From here Bernadette saw the Virgin and prayed." Near by knelt devout Hungarians 200 strong, headed by a Bishop and thirteen Priests, all singing in unison a plain chant Mass. Oh! how pious, how animated, how solemn and how devotional was the very atmosphere of the place! One of the pilgrims, a paralytic for many years who was carried on a stretcher, was instantaneously cured by bathing in the holy spring.

In the evening of that first day I visited the great Basilica and the splendid Church of the Rosary, with its fifteen highly ornamented chapels representing the fifteen mysteries of the Rosary.

While rambling on the banks of the Gave under the lofty trees so well known to the pilgrims, I met an old Priest who saluted me by my name. It was Rev. Father Domenech, a missionary whom I had met in Galveston at Bishop Odin's residence in the year 1852. He is the author of several books, some of which relate to missionary life and doings in Texas and Mexico. They are well written and highly interesting, but they are too romantic to deserve the name of history. Gilmary Shea, the historian of the Catholic Church in the United States, calls them "extravagant."

The news of the arrival of Cardinal Langenieux, Archbishop of Rheims, accompanied by the Bishop of Tarbes and 100 seminarians, was announced, and pilgrims by the hundreds gathered at the basilica. The following day His Eminence celebrated Mass, and the seminarians executed in a masterly manner a beautiful and soul-stirring solemn Mass in Gregorian chant. Oh! how that church music speaks to the heart and elevates the soul! There were no solos, no duets to act as dampers on the devotion of the pious assistants. The Amen was never sung twice. Too often modern church music serves only to tickle the ear and stifle devotion.

Two days in Lourdes was the time fixed upon for my stay in that city of wonders, but as new pilgrimages were constantly arriving, and new prodigies were in expectation, I resolved to prolong my sojourn in order to see the praying multitude, and enjoy the pious atmosphere so well known and appreciated by the devout pilgrims.

I can never forget the delight of those specimens of suffering humanity, declared incurable by the medical faculty; men, women and children with bandages or wadding on their wounds and sores—cancerous for the most part—and nearly all carried on hand-barrows, stretchers or hand carts. There was the consumptive, the blind, the deaf, the cripple, the paralytic, and some apparently were in their agony.

I was told of two cases which had baffled medical science and experience. The first case was that of a young lady from Paris, the only daughter of pious and rich parents. She was in the last stage of consumption. When she was apprised of her approaching dissolution, she exclaimed: "To see our Lady of Lourdes and die." Doctors were consulted and they declared she was too weak to undertake the long journey and might die on the road. She prevailed on her father to let her go, and he was not able to refuse this last favor to his dying child. Mattresses and other precautionary appliances were soon in readiness for the perilous enterprise. With great anxiety and difficulty Lourdes was reached. Fervent prayers were recited and the girl was carried into the piscina. When, behold! She came out of the sacred font perfectly cured, and she, who for eighteen months had been bed-ridden and unable to taste of any solid food, went on foot to the basilica where she remained kneeling for a quarter of an hour. Then she repaired to her hotel, accompanied by her father and mother, where she partook of a hearty breakfast.

The other case was declared a hopeless one and beyond the reach of the medical faculty. The sick man entered the piscina; prayers went up to Mary, and the sick man came out of the water instantaneously cured.

The doctors had declared the man incurable, but one of them exclaimed: "He is certainly cured, no one can deny it; by what agent we know not, but certainly not by any natural agency."

The miraculous cures at Lourdes are reckoned by thousands. They are well attested; they are facts that cannot be denied except by infidels or by disciples of the Pharisees of old, who, being unable to deny supernatural facts, attributed them to Beelzebub, the prince of devils.

A man might as well turn his face to the Sun at noonday and deny that it shines, as to look upon Lourdes with its wonderful history and development and say that it is not what it is claimed to be—a living testimony to the power of God, manifested through the Blessed Virgin Mary.

The apparition of Lourdes confirms our Catholic faith. It is a historical fact that the numerous apparitions of the Queen of Heaven on this sphere, and her myriads of supernatural interventions in human affairs, were uniformly in behalf of the Catholic Church. Who ever heard of a miracle or of a supernatural apparition in favor of the numberless sects? Outside of the Church, Mary is not invoked.

St. Thomas Aquinas asks the question: "Could the Almighty God create worlds and creatures more perfect than those that actually exist?" and answers it: "Yes, excepting the humanity of Jesus Christ, Heaven and the Blessed Virgin Mary." St. Augustine says equally of these three creatures that "God has exhausted his science, his power, and his goodness," saying, "Plus dare nescivit. Plus dare non potuit. Plus dare non habuit." Imagine, now, what may be the greatness and the power of Mary. "All good comes through Mary," says St. Bernard.

When I visited the Grande Chartreuse, the Superior General told me that the solemn baptism and reception into the Church of an English lady, an Episcopalian, was to take place at La Salette the next day. These were the circumstances of her conversion. The lady in question was an invalid who had for many years, sought in vain, relief from the most celebrated doctors in London, when she resolved to come to La Salette saying: "If I recover my health through the intercession of Mary, I promise and vow to join the Catholic Church." After two novenas of prayers, she was radically cured. Faithful to her promise, she was instructed by a Bishop, received conditional baptism, made her First Communion, and was confirmed, all on the same day. After a six days' sojourn, I left Lourdes with supreme regret.

Oh! land of beauty, of holiness; no wonder that man's soul on thy fair bosom and beneath thy golden skies, feels itself lifted up to the Creator and pours forth its love and worship in ecstatic hymns. Adieu, adieu! We passed through Marseilles where many years ago I had received the unction of the priesthood from the hands of the saintly Bishop Monseigneur, Joseph Eugene de Mazenod, the founder of the Oblates of Mary Immaculate, whose cause of beatification is in preparation. From that city we passed through Monaco, the smallest of the independent principalities of Europe, on the Mediterranean. The army consists of five officers and seventy men. Hail Genoa, the birth place of St. Catherine! San Marino, the oldest independent republic of the world, is soon reached. It is said to have been founded early in the fourth century by the monk St. Marinus. We passed the night at Ancona. The next day we said Mass at Loretto, in the house formerly inhabited by the Holy Family.

CHAPTER XII.

Loretto. A Soldier Says Mass. History of the Translation of the Holy House. Proofs of the Miracle.

The comfort of modern railway traveling cannot give an adequate idea of a pilgrimage. We should have felt more like real pilgrims had we slowly and painfully climbed the blue Appennines on foot, with staff and scrip; but our faith was in no way lessened, even though we went to Loretto by rail, and did not toil along the highway, or over the mountain passes. We can never forget the first glimpse of the green, smiling hillside of Loretto, rising so majestically against the blue sky. The feelings of the heart cannot be described, as one gazes for the first time at Loretto, and strives to realize that under yon noble dome stands the cottage of the Holy Family. We hastened to enter the Basilica and to pass under the portal over which is written the inscription: "The house of the Mother of God wherein the Word was made flesh." Within the Basilica is seen the Holy House, the dwelling place of the Son of God and His Virgin Mother, for so many years.

A pilgrimage to Loretto had been for a long time the object of our ardent desires, and when the long-looked for opportunity came at last, how joyously we ascended the hillside of that privileged city to Loretto, where Kings, Cardinals and Popes have lowered their dignity and cast aside all earthly pomp, to go and kneel as humble pilgrims under the roof of the Virgin of Nazareth and kiss the walls which heard the first "Ave Maria," and within which "the Word was made flesh!"

The day previous we had arranged, by telegram, the hours for our Masses in the Holy House. Very Rev. Father McGrath, O. M. I., late provincial of the United

States province of the Oblates, and Father Lefebvre, now provincial O. M. I., and myself had our time fixed from 7 to 8:30. Exactly at 8 o'clock I was vesting for my Mass when there came a soldier who asked me if I would not allow him to say Mass in my place, as he was in a hurry to regain his regiment. I saw at once that he was a soldier-Priest in the service of "Umberto." For Priests, like laymen, were obliged to serve their time in the army, an evil which still exists in some of the nations of Europe. Of course, I gave him my place, and commenced my Mass at 8:30. But oh! how can I express my sentiments, my feelings, my enthusiasm, during that hour. "The Son of God was made flesh in this very house, in the womb of the Blessed Virgin Mary, over eighteen centuries ago, and I, a poor missionary, in the same place cause the same Son of God made flesh to descend from heaven and come into my hands. O Mystery!"

Although the history of the translation of the "Holy House" is well known by many, yet, for the information of others who may not be so favored regarding the particulars of this stupendous prodigy, I shall relate as briefly as possible the facts of this marvel:

On the morning of May 12, 1291, some wood-cutters went to work on a little hill called Raunissa, between Fiume and Tersatto in Dalmatia, and where there was nothing but an open space the evening before, they saw a house surmounted by a belfry containing two small bells. The sight of it filled them with awe and astonishment, especially when they observed that it had no foundations, but was simply resting on the soil where it had been laid down during the night. After a while when they became bold enough to enter it, they found that it was to all intents a little chapel, with an altar, a crucifix, a statue of the Blessed Virgin, etc. We can easily imagine the commotion created in the neighboring towns and villages as the news spread. Astonishment changed into veneration when their worthy pastor, Alexander, appeared among the people and declared to them the mystery of the Holy House. Our Lady appeared to him and assured him that it was no other than her House from Nazareth. "There," she said, "I was born; there the Son of God was made man, and lived with me for a long time; and there, after His glorious Ascension, the august Sacrifice was offered up by the Apostles. To remove this sanctuary from the profanation of the infidels, God had it transported to this place." The Blessed Virgin then freed him from his malady, a dropsy of three years' standing, and commanded him to go immediately to venerate her earthly home. His very appearance among the people prepared them for the revelation he had to make known to them, a truth which bore the stamp of verity on it, confirmed by the miracle of his restoration to health. Veneration for the Holy House was thereby intensified, and the joy at possessing such a treasure was great, indeed.

At that time a noble Roman, named Nicholas Frangipani, was Lord of Tersatto and Governor of Slavonia and Croatia for the Austrian Emperor, Rudolph I. When he heard of the prodigy of the arrival of the Holy House; he visited the spot, and, after considering it attentively, knelt down in holy reverence. Wishing to employ all human means to ascertain the truth of the miraculous translation, he chose four delegates and sent them to Nazareth with the measurements of the Holy House. Comparisons of cement and materials all showed the foundations at Nazareth to agree in every particular with the house at Tersatto.

When they questioned the few Christians who yet remained in Nazareth, the story they told of the disappearance of the Holy House put it beyond all doubt that it was the treasure which had come to them. The documents proving all this were deposited in the public Archives of Tersatto.

But on the 10th of December, 1294, three years and seven months after its appearance in Dalmatia, the Holy House again took flight across one hundred and forty miles of sea and landed in the marshes of Ancona, in Italy. It rested near the shores of the Adriatic. Some shepherds watching their flocks in the territory of Recanati, beheld a house, which seemed to be carried by invisible hands, crossing the sea to them in the early dawn. It gradually descended into a little wood about a mile and a half from the shore. The news soon spread abroad, and, as before, the Blessed Virgin chose her special messengers to confirm the truth. These were St. Nicholas de Tolentino and the hermit, Paul de Selva.

Soon the fame of the shrine attracted many pilgrims, who brought rich gifts, and the place being solitary, it soon became the haunt of robbers and assassins.

For the third time the Holy House was mysteriously conveyed from its resting place and it suddenly made its appearance upon an eminence near the public road that leads to Recanati. The owners of this place were two rich brothers, Counts Stephen and Simon Rinaldo de Antici, who, being devout and God fearing men, were overjoyed at finding such a treasure on their property. But when they realized that they might become wealthy by reason of the great concourse of pilgrims and the rich offerings they made, greed of gold so stifled their sentiments of piety and brotherly love that they quarrelled over the possession of the sanctuary site and the division of the spoils. To put an end to this unseemly contest and to make the Holy House accessible to all, the municipal authorities of Recanati sent a petition to Rome to have the site declared common property. Before an answer was received, Heaven itself settled the difficulty in a manner they little expected, for, the Holy House was again miraculously transferred, months later, to the public highway, where it stands to-day a stone's throw from its former position.

Such is the abridged history of the translations of Holy House of Loretto. Its history and its wonders have occupied the attention of long ages and deserve more than a superficial study.

To dismiss with a smart saying or to deny the miracle of the repeated translations would be to dismiss and deny one of the best attested historical facts. Few historical facts are backed by so many traditions, documents and moral proofs. To account for its existence in Loretto without admitting a miracle, is impossible. To maintain that it was brought over by human hands would complicate and multiply without lessening the miracle. To prove a second time its identity with that of Tersatto and Nazareth, a committee of sixteen men were sent in the year 1296, at the public expense. The stones and mortar when analysed were shown to be the same as those in common use in Nazareth and quite different from those found in or about the marshes of Ancona. The very fact that it stands without foundations has been admitted by competent architects to be sufficient proof that it was not built on its present site by human hands. Before the tribunal of those who regard miracles as proof of imposture, the Holy House of Loretto must protest very strongly. To one who has not the faith it must seem an improbable tale, worthy of the "Arabian Nights." "Were there no truth in the whole story," says a modern writer on Loretto, "then it would be a series of wholesale deception, of inexplicable events, of superhuman trickery, impossible to have been invented.

executed and maintained for centuries; a thing far more extraordinary than all we explain by angelical agency."

CHAPTER XIII.

Rome. First Impressions. The Quirinal. My Cicerone. The Obelisk. Fontana. The Colonnade. St. Peter's Church. Michael Angelo. The Cupola. The Confession.

Hail city of the Pope!! Behold that beautiful dome, yonder, high up in the air!! How magnificent the surrounding historical hills, with their ancient palaces and villas, exquisitely constructed for the kings and emperors of old! These ruins speak of past grandeur! There stands the Coliseum where so many noble, pure and innocent Christian heroes were sacrificed to wild beasts to satiate the horrid thirst of Nero for the blood of Christians!! Here stands the well preserved Arch of Titus surrounded by the newly discovered truncated columns and arches! There is the Roman Forum! I beheld around me the monumental history of twenty-five centuries. On the ruins of ancient and pagan Rome is built the Rome of the Popes, the Eternal City. The immortal Peter is there, though a prisoner by the hands of iniquity. Eleven times he has been brutally driven out of the Holy City, and ten times he has returned triumphantly to his Estates.

There is the Pope's palace where the conclaves were held for the election of the Popes. In this palace there is a spacious dining hall which is called the hall of canonization. Now, this palace is occupied by a robber King, a worthy son of his sire. While standing in front of the Quirinal built by Gregory XIII, Sixtus V, and Clement VIII, I recalled the atrocities committed within its walls against Pius VII by order of Napoleon the First, and against Pius IX by modern infidels occupying high places. The Psalm, "Quare fremuerunt gentes" flashed into my mind as I continued my way through the city. "The kings of the earth stood up against the Lord saying: Let us break his bonds asunder and let us cast away his yoke from us. But He shall rule them with a rod of iron and break them in pieces."

As my sojourn in the Eternal City was limited to twenty-one days, I used my time to the best advantage. Therefore I looked first to my spiritual interests in saying my Mass every day in one or other of the principal Basilicas or Sanctuaries, and then devoted all the available moments of the day to visiting Rome, its monuments, and places of interest.

In order to accomplish this twofold end, I felt the need of a good "Cicerone." The Very Reverend Cassien Augier, who, at the time was the Oblates' General Procurator in Rome, and who is now the Superior General of the Congregation, showed me a kindness and rendered me a service which I shall never forget. One of our students, a Roman by the name of D' Eramo, was immediately dispensed from his regular studies and placed at my call any time I might require his services. This young man knew all the nooks and corners of the city, and every day at the fixed hours I invariably found the young "Cicerone" at the gate with a hack ready to take me through the city.

My first visit was devoted to a superficial view of St. Peter's Church and the Vatican. Three subsequent visits completed the notes which I now transcribe.

The immense "piazza" in front of St. Peter's Basilica is adorned with an Obelisk, the only one which has been preserved entire, and which was transported from Heliopolis by order of Caligula. It is one hundred and twenty-four feet in height and was erected by Sixtus the Fifth under the direction of Fontana, who, to raise it out of the earth in which it lay buried, contrived forty-one machines, and though all the powers of these machines was applied at once by means of eight hundred men and one hundred and sixty horses, it took over eight days to accomplish the stupendous work; and to transport the Obelisk to the place where it now stands, though only three hundred paces from the spot where it lay, it required four months' labor. But the greatest proof of Fontana's skill in mechanics was displayed when he erected this ponderous mass and fixed it in its present position by the aid of fifty-two machines, all of which were applied at the same moment. When set at its proper height it was placed, without any cement, on the backs of four lions, amidst the acclamations of the people and the discharge of cannon from the castle of San Angelo. Its own ponderosity is sufficient to prevent it from falling. Report says, however, that Fontano nearly failed in the end, because the ropes having stretched much more than he expected, the Obelisk could not have been raised high enough to be placed on its pedestal, had not a sailor named Bresca, at the time when every spectator was restricted from speaking under the severest penalty, called out, in defiance of this order: "Acqua alle fune," "Wet the ropes." When this was done the Obelisk was immediately raised to its destined height. This enormous monolith weighs 893,537 pounds.

Two beautiful fountains adorn the piazza; one was erected by Innocent VII and the other by Clement VIII. The colonnades were built during the Pontificate of Alexander VII. They are the admiration of all visitors. Their form is semi-circular, and they consist of 284 large columns, interspersed with eighty-eight pilasters, and form on each side of the piazza a tripple portico, the center one of which is wide enough for two carriages to pass one another. The height of these colonnades is 61 feet, and on the entablature is a balustrade adorned with

292 statues, each being eleven feet and a half in height. Beyond the colonnades are two magnificent covered galleries, 360 feet long, leading to the vestibule of the Basilica, which stands on the summit of a noble flight of steps. The vestibule is 439 feet long by 37 feet wide and contains equestrian statues of Constantine and Charlemagne at each end. Five doors open into the Basilica.

On entering, I exclaimed; "Is this St. Peter's Basilica? Is this the most magnificent, the grandest church in the world? Is this in reality, the masterpiece of human genius?" I looked disappointed..... "Father," said one of my companions who was already well acquainted with Rome and its monuments. "Do you see yonder those statues of angels which support that marble holy water font? How high do you think they are?" "Well," I replied, "they look to be three feet." "Let us go near them," said he. As we advanced nearer and nearer, the statues appeared to become higher and higher, until, to our surprise, we found them to be seven feet high. Our Cicerone then told us a story about a certain English lady who with her husband was visiting St. Peter's. Becoming fatigued, she told her husband that she would like to go and sit down on what appeared in the distance to be a low bench. But when she reached the bench, she found to her dismay that it would require a ladder to reach it. So admirably proportioned is this church, that, notwithstanding its immense size, no one, at first sight perceives the magnitude of its dimensions.

Our admiration increased at every step. An attempt at description is out of the question. The interior of this wondrous temple is incrusted with rare and beautiful marble, adorned with the finest existing pictures in mosaic; the statues are numberless, and are the work of great masters. The number of columns and pilasters is very great. The pavement is in rich marble and very handsome. The length of the largest churches in Chrtstendom is marked by gold stars incrusted in the pavement. The first we examine gives the length of St. Paul's, London. In looking back towards the doors, the distance that is in excess of St. Paul's would make a grand church by itself. The next star indicates the length of the Duomo of Florence. Then comes the Cathedrals of Milan and of Bologna, then the stars showing the length of St. Paul's, outside of Rome, then Our Lady of Antwerp and lastly St. Sophia of Constantinople, which star is not far from the gigantic pillars upon which rests the dome of St. Peter's. We are now under the immense cupola, the heart of the stupendous work of Michael Angelo. We now understand the words of a corypheus of the infidel philosophers of the last century, "Under St. Peter's dome I become a believer." Far up at the four corners of the cupola are the four evangelists twenty-two feet high. The pen which St. Luke holds in his hand is six feet long. Let us now go up into the dome and inspect that miracle of architecture. There are two galleries inside and around the dome. The height from the pavement to the first gallery is 194 feet and to the second 270 feet. We reach those galleries through narrow openings in the rotunda. But oh! Who can look down on the pavement below without trembling! Very few dare go around the dome because the galleries are slender and narrow. These words, "Thou art Peter and upon this rock I will build my Church, and I will give unto thee the keys of the kingdom of heaven" are written in mosaic around the interior of the dome. They are seven feet high although when seen from the pavement below they appear to be only one foot. The height from the pavement to the lantern where the Eternal Father is represented in mosaic is 417 feet. We now come down and take another direction to make our ascent to the ball above the cupola and under the cross, the highest point attainable. We ascend a staircase, consisting of 142 steps, by which mules might mount, so easy is the ascent. We arrived at the immense platform on top of the church, at the foot of the great dome, where the workmen and artists of the Basilica live with their families in beautiful residences. Here we met the custodian of the dome, who asked us to show our permit. We began the ascent through narrow and winding staircases till we arrived below the ball, where as many as seventeen visitors may be admitted at the same time. The ladder leading to the ball is of iron and nearly perpendicular. The aparture through which one has to pass, is of small dimensions, and can safely admit only those of ordinary rotundity. My two companions, more careful than I, remained at the foot of the ladder. After casting a rapid glance around the ball through small windows, and enjoying the beautiful panorama below, I quickly left the place and went down to join my companions, for the heat in the ball was so oppressive that I feared being suffocated.

Under St. Peter's is a subterranean church about twelve or thirteen feet high. The chapel which contains the body of St. Peter is just under the high altar. We descended to that crypt by a very fine marble staircase. The corridors and chapels are all highly ornamented with mosaic statues and candelabra. The light of day never enters into these long corridors and chapels. I had the happy opportunity of offering up the Holy Sacrifice of the Mass near the body of St. Peter. Ninety-three lamps are continually kept burning around the relics of St. Peter. They are extinguished only on Good Friday.

CHAPTER XIV.

The Vitican. The Mamertine Prison. The Catacombs. St. Stanislaus Kotzka. Montorio. The Pincio. St. Peter and St. Paul. Separation.

This palace of the Popes is the greatest in the universe. It contains 11,000 rooms. There are eight enormous marble staircases and two hundred of minor dimensions. Near the gardens of the Vatican, there is a neat little village containing the residences of those employed in the Pontifical post-office and of the secretaries of the twenty Roman Congregations with their workmen and servants. There also reside the Swiss and the Noble Guards and over five thousand men who are employed in the numerous departments of the Papel government. Wagon loads of mail matter, from the four quarters of the globe, daily pour into the Vatican. Its museum is the most considerable in the world; so is the library with its immense collection of manuscripts. The palace contains twenty court yards.

Under the church of St. Peter in Carcere is an ancient prison called the Mamertine; it is well worth seeing, though cold and damp. St. Peter and Paul were confined here for eight months. Above the church of St. Peter in Carcere is another church, called St. Joseph of the Carpenters. Going down through these two churches, which are one above the other, a long flight of stairs leads us to a dark crypt of elliptical form. From this gloomy place we descend into the Mamertine prison, which is still more sombre. It has no windows, a small aperture in the vault above was formerly the only opening through which the prisoners were let down. A staircase was built in the beginning of this century, for the convenience of pilgrims. Near a small column is a spring of water which issued forth miraculously at the prayer of

St. Peter that he might baptize the two jailors, Processus and Martinianus, and forty-seven other prisoners, all of whom afterwards suffered martyrdom. It was then that the light of charity, for the first time, penetrated into this dark and horrid dungeon. With difficulty, I obtained permission to say Mass in that hideous cold, and excessively damp hole, sanctified by the first martyrs of Catholic faith. This gave me an idea of the Catacombs. The evening of the same day saw me in the church of St. Agnes outside the walls of Rome. After having visited the relics of the beautiful young virgin lying under the high altar: the Saint, beloved above all by the Romans, we entered the Catacombs. We were five, each furnished with a lighted torch, and led by a guide. It was often necessary to stoop while going through these caverns, but, generally speaking, they are neither very damp nor difficult of access. The passages are from two to three feet wide. In the walls are cavities, many of which are open and empty, others closed with a piece of marble, sometimes containing an inscription. Sometimes a monogram, signifying "Pro Christo," is found upon a monument. This is deemed a sure indication of a martyr's sepulchre. A cross on a monument is also considered as a sign that a Christian lies buried there. The extent of these Catacombs cannot be accurately known, because it is impoosible to explore every part of them, as their communications with each other are so intricate that several persons have been lost in these subterranean labyrinths. While visiting these necropolises, crypts, and subterranean sanctuaries I fancied myself living in the first centuries of the Catholic Church. At every step we met ancient monuments or symbols giving evidence that the Church was in the first centuries, what she is now and will be unto the end of time, the work of God, unchangeable, unalterable and indefectible. "Behold," said Christ, "I am with you all days even to the consummation of the world." Of two things it may be said with absolute certainty that they will rise to-morrow: The Sun and the Catholic Church.

My next Mass was celebrated in the beautiful church of St. Ignatius, on the altar of St. Aloysias Gonzaga. The urn containing his relics is of lapis lazuli. Near the church is the Roman College, the greatest establishment of public instruction in the city of Rome. There I visited the rooms once occupied by St. Aloysius Gonzaga and by St. John Berchmans. The students from Mexico and South America follow the full course of ecclasiastical studies in this celebrated university. They are a very intelligent gathering of young clerics.

On the following day I said Mass on the tomb of St. Ignatius of Loyola in the church of "di Gesu." Above the altar, in a niche trimmed with lapis lazuli, is a large statue of St. Ignatius accompanied by angels. The remains of the Saint repose under the altar, I made my thanksgiving after Mass at the altar of St. Francis Xavier, where his right arm and hand are seen. On the two following days I had the good fortune of saying Mass in the rooms of St. Aloysius Gonzaga and St. Stanislaus Kostka. Near the altar of St. Stanislaus is his statue which represents the saint reclining on his death bed, in the very spot where he rendered his spotless soul into the hands of his Creator. This statue is considered a masterpiece. The head, hands, and feet are of the purest white marble. The expression is admirable. The body of the Saint is covered with a sombre blanket. To be certain that this is marble and not a woolen fabric, it is necessary to touch it with the hand, the illusion is so perfect.

One beautiful Sunday evening we visited Montorio,

where St. Peter was crucified, and St. Paul of the Three Fountains; where St. Paul suffered martyrdom. The hill of Montorio is extremely picturesque. From the terrace in front of the church we enjoyed the magnificent panorama of the city, the mountains of Latium and the plains extending beyond St. Paul outside the walls.

Near the church of Montorio there is a convent of Franciscan Friars, where an elegant little round temple, a master-piece of Bramante is to be seen. It is a cupola supported by sixteen columns of black granite and covers the place where the cross, on which the Prince of the Apostles died, was erected. A few paces from Montorio and on the Janiculum heights is the Pauline Fountain, a monument worth seeing. It was erected by Paul V. When we arrived at the end of the Janiculum hill, we enjoyed a spectacle which I shall never forget. Before us stood St. Peter's and the Vatican in all their splendor and magnificence. Crossing St. Peter's piazza and the bridge of St. Angelo, we passed in front of the Fountain of Trevi, the most sumptuous in Rome and perhaps the largest in the world. When we arrived in front of the Quirinal, one of my companions humorously asked me how I should like to go and offer my respects to King Umberto. "I had rather wait," I replied, "until he gets out of Rome and restores his ill-gotten goods." We rode through the Roman Forum and reached the Pincio and the Villa Borghese, a most beautiful park of four and a half miles in circumference, adorned with lakes, fountains and a great number of marble statues. From the terrace we enjoyed another excellent panorama of the city. This is the rendezvous of the Roman nobility, who are to be seen riding there every afternoon in sumptuous carriages with uniformed drivers and lackeys.

From there a drive of four miles brought us to St.

Paul of the Three Fountains, the place where the Apostle St. Paul was beheaded.

From the Mamertine prison, where they had been kept during eight months, St. Peter and St. Paul, on the day when they were to be executed, walked forth together between two companies of soldiers. On the road they met St. Plautilla., a noble Roman lady, who, in tears, had come to meet the holy Apostles, marching to their places of execution. After consoling the lady, one of his numerous converts, St. Paul asked for her veil in order to cover his eyes with it at the moment of his execution. A short distance from here is seen another small edifice called the Chapel of Separation, erected on the spot where the Apostles exchanged the last kiss of peace before separating; St. Peter being led to the Janiculum, and St. Paul to the Aquae Salviae, now St. Paul of the Three Fountains.

CHAPTER XV.

St. John Lateran. The Scala Santa. St. Mary Major. St. Paul. St. Benedict Labre. Holy Cross of Jerusalem. Domine Quo Vadis? St. Peter's Chains.

On entering this church the visitor is struck by the magnificence and majesty of the middle nave. Although there are defects in the details, yet the general aspect is pleasing. The Basilica of St. John Lateran, possesses, from its origin, a prominence which it still enjoys. Saint Sylvester ennobled it with the title of the "episcopal church of the Roman Pontiff." It is here that the Popes used, until lately, to take possession of their see. As the authority of the supreme head of the universal Church is inherited in the office of successor of St. Peter, vicar of Jesus Christ and Bishop of Rome, the episcopal Church of Rome or Saint John Lateran is the first of all the churches of Rome and of the whole world. The following inscriptions may be seen on its walls: "Sacrosancta Lateranensis ecclesia omnium urbis et orbis Mater et caput."

The treasury of this church contains the following precious relics: The table on which our savior instituted the Holy Eucharist, (in close proximity to which it has been my happy lot to offer the Holy sacrifice of the Mass); one arm of St. Helena; the cup in which, by order of Diocletian, poison was presented to the apostle St. John; a part of the chain with which he was bound when brought from Ephesus to Rome; a piece of the scarlet cloak that was put about Jesus Christ, in derision; the heads of Sts. Peter and Paul.

The Scala Santa is the staircase of Pontius Pilate's palace in Jerusalem which our Savior ascended and descended four times on the morning of his Passion. It has twenty-eight steps. St. Helena ordered it to be brought from Jerusalem to Rome. It is in a church erected near the church of St. John Lateran. The pilgrims ascend that holy staircase on their knees and gain several indulgences. There may be seen on three of the steps stains of the Divine blood protected by glass.

The obelisk on the plaza of St. John Lateran is the highest of the eleven that embelish the various piazzas of Rome. This monolith is 142 feet high, and was transported from Heliopolis, in the year 357.

The Basilica of St. Mary's Major owes its origin to the miracle of the snow on August 5, in the beginning of the fourth century. In this church is preserved the cradle of the infant Jesus, transported from Palestine A. D. 642, together with the body of St. Jerome. These precious relics are deposited in the chapel of the Crucifix where I had the happiness of offering the Sacrafice of the Mass. Here my young "Cicerone" played a trick on me. He left me to go and visit his uncle, a Canon of the Basilica who lived close by. "I shall be back in a few minutes," said he. But he delayed so long that I had time to meditate on the "eternal years" and visit the church in all its details before he came back. Here are the tombs of St. Pius V. Clement VIII, and Paul V.

St. Lucine. a noble Roman lady, of a senatorial family, and a disciple of St. Paul, possessed a villa where she deposited the body of her master, on the spot where now stands the sumptuous Basilica of St. Paul outside the walls.

On the 16th of July 1823 St. Paul's church was destroyed by fire. It was rebuilt by Leo XII, Gregory XVI and Pius IX. On the 10th. of December 1854 it was solemnly consecrated by Pius IX in the presence of 185 Cardinals and Bishops who had come to Rome for the definition of the dogma of the Immaculate Conception. Their names may be seen on two marble slabs inserted in the walls of the apsis of this Basilica. How pleased I felt when I read there the name of the founder of the Oblates of Mary Immaculate, Charles Joseph Engene de Mazenod.

In the Basilica of St. Lawrence outside the walls may be seen the monument erected over the remains of Pius IX. The only inscription seen on this mausoleum is the following: "Ossa et cineres Pii IX" The next Mass I celebrated was over the body of the most extraordinary Saint of these latter times, St. Benedict Labre. Who was he? A personage illustrious by his birth or by his wealth? A learned man? No. He was apparently a vulgar and worthless individual, covered with rags and barefooted, who voluntarily reduced himself to the condition of a poor beggar, without a dwelling place. He left his comfortable home in France to visit all the principal sanctuaries of Italy, and finally settled in Rome where for fourteen years he slept on a stone bench under one of the arches of the Coliseum. His was a life of penance and prayer. He begged for his food and gave to his fellow-beggars the best morsels he received, reserving for himself a few raw vegetables or some decayed fruit. His principal occupation was to visit the churches where the Blessed Sacrament was exposed, and there to remain in contemplation for hours. Such a life is beyond the comprehension of this sensual and voluptuous epoch.

This church of the Holy cross of Jerusalem derives its name from part of the true cross which St. Helena brought from Jerusalem and deposited here with other precious relics, which are: One of the nails which held our Savior to the cross, two thorns of the crown of our Blessed Lord, the finger which St. Thomas put in the wounds of Jesus, ("Put in thy finger hither," said Christ, "and be not incredulous,") the title of the cross I. N. R. I. We had the privilege of being shown these sacred relics, which are publicly exposed only on the fourth Sunday in Lent, on Good Friday, and on the 3rd of May.

This church, "Quo Vadis," is situated on the Appian way where St. Peter by the advice of the Christians, was fleeing from the persecution of Nero, when our Savior appeared to him. "Lord" said St. Peter, "where are you going?" "I go to Rome," answered Jesus, "there to be crucified anew." St. Peter at once retraced his steps, and remained in Rome, until he suffered martyrdom on the cross.

When St. Peter was arrested and kept in prison by order of Herod he was bound with two chains. An angel of the Lord appeared to him and said: "Arise quickly" "and the chains fell off from his hands." (Acts chap. xii.) These chains were religiously kept in Jerusalem by the Christians.

In the year 436 the Empress Eudoxia, wife of Theodose the younger, having visited Jerusalem, obtained these chains from Juvenal, Bishop of the city, and sent them to her daughter Eudoxia, wife of the Emperor Valentinian. At that time the church in Rome possessed another chain with which St. Peter had been bound by order of Nero. Pope St. Leo, having received the precious gift from Eudoxia, put the two chains near one another when behold! they were miraculously joined together so as to form only one chain. In honor of St. Peter and in memory of this prodigy, the Pope and Eudoxia erected the Church of St. Peter's chains, which also bears the name of the Eudoxian Basilica. Four links from the chain of St. Paul have been added to that of St. Peter. A solemn feast is celebrated in the whole Catholic world on the first of August, in honor of this memorable event. It was my happy fortune to say Mass on the altar where these chains are preserved.

St. Peter came to Rome in the year 42 and lived there twenty-five years. This is an historical fact. How is it that some Protestant writers deny it? Should any one deny that the Sun is shining, this denial, although repeated 10,000 times, would not be able to blot out the old planet from the firmament.

CHAPTER XVI.

In Rome, the Stones Speak. Audience of the Pope. Pause. The Gates of Hell Shall Not Prevail.

In Rome the stones speak. My next Mass was celebrated in the baths of Saint Cecilia, on the very stone where this beautiful and noble virgin was decapitated. This altar was never consecrated, except by the blood of the holy martyr.

The Church of St. Praxedes possesses the column

to which our Saviour was bound during his cruel flagellation. Close to that precious relic it was my good fortune to say Mass. In that Basilica are the remains of 2300 martyrs taken from the catacombs, and deposited here by Pascal I. In a collateral chapel is seen a long marble slab on which is read the following inscription: "On this marble stone the Virgin Praxedes was wont to sleep." In the center of the church is a well where Praxedes used to bury the remains of martyrs.

On the piazza Scossa Cavalle is the church of St. James, where are seen two stones brought to Rome by St. Helena. Tradition has it that on one of these stones Abraham placed his son Isaac, to sacrifice him to the Lord. On the other stone the Blessed Virgin on the day of the Presentation in the temple, placed the Infant Jesus, the true Isaac, the victim of the new dispensation. In the catacombs; in the recent excavations; in the mosaics, paintings and statuary, we have the history of the church in marble and stone. There is the history of the supremacy of St. Peter and his successors, Saints Linus, Cletus, Clement, etc. There is the history of the seven Sacraments, of the intercession of the Saints, of the Mass and Confession during the first four centuries of the Church. The Church of God does not change. "You change, therefore you err," says Bossuet, in his celebrated "Variations," addressed to the numberless sects of dissenters. True Catholics feel at home in Rome. In a few days they travel over nineteen centuries, and like the first Christians, are ready to shed their blood for the "one God, one faith, one baptism." Relying on Christ's promise: "Behold, I am with you all days, even to the consummation of the world," they are never troubled by the least shadow of a doubt.

The audience of the Pope was fixed a few days previous by the Monsignore Maestro di Camara, for 4 o'clock p. m. We were all gathered near the Pope's apartments at the given hour.

When the Pope appeared accompanied by the Monsignore Majordomo and two of the Noble Guards, twenty-seven Oblate Fathers fell on their knees to receive the first blessing of the Vicar of Christ on earth. The majestic appearance of the Pope filled our minds with awe and profound veneration. Here was the immortal Peter, the center of unity, the mouth-piece of the Almighty, and the infallible teacher of mankind. "I prayed for thee, Peter, that thy faith fail not; confirm thy brethren."

We must believe firmly that the prayer of our Saviour was heard; therefore, the faith of Peter has not failed and is exercised by his successors to the end of time.

The Pope had a good word for each one of us. Very Rev. Father McGrath, the late Provincial of the Province in the United States had asked me to address the Pope in French, and to ask his Holiness certain faculties. When the Pope approached me he said: "And you, Father, where is your mission?" "In Texas, Holy Father." "Ah! a hard mission; zeal and perseverance, my son." This was the moment to ask for the faculties. So, taking the hand of His Holiness and pressing it, "Holy Father," I said, "May I ask of your Holiness a favor?" "Yes; my son, what is it?" "The faculty of giving the Papal Benediction, on our return, in all the churches of our province." "Oh, my son you ask too much." Then perceiving the movement of the Pope towards the next Priest, I added: "Holy Father, may I ask your Holiness the faculty for three churches only?" "Ah, this is more reasonable; where is your Provincial?" "Here, Holy Father, I replied, pointing to Father McGrath. "Father Provincial," said the Pope,

"I give you the faculty of giving the Papal Benediction in three of your churches, but only once in each church." After receiving the last blessing of the Pope, we retired.

* * * * * * * *

Here I must pause. I had seen Rome with its crumbling monuments of antiquity; I had seen paganism and its thousands of idols buried under the debris of ages. Where is ancient Rome? Where is the Roman Empire, that colossus bestriding the earth? The poor fisherman of Galilee has conquered it. Is this the work of man? The works of man begin, progress, flourish, decline and die. Where are now to be found the Arians, the Manicheans, the Pelagians, the Nestorians, the Albigenses? They disturbed the Church for a time. They are dead and their work has perished with them. Protestantism is on the decline, weakened by its 300 discordant sects. It may continue to protest against the Church of God for a time, but it will finally disappear from the face of the world. And why? Because it is the work of men. The Church of Rome will endure to the end of time, because it is the work of God. We rest the issue on the words of the Pharisee Gamaliel, a doctor of the law. "And now, therefore, I say to you, refrain from these men, and let them alone; for if this design or work be of men, it will fall to nothing: but if it be of God, you are not able to destroy it; lest perhaps you be found to oppose God." (Acts of the Apostles, chapter v, verses 38, 39.) It is useless to fight against God and His Church. "For the gates of hell shall not prevail against it." The words of Julian, the Apostate, "Thou hast conquered, O Galilean!" shall resound until doomsday.

"But the scandals in the Catholic Church; the scandals in Rome!" If there were no scandals it would be a miracle. Our Saviour says: "It must needs be that scandal come, but nevertheless, woe to that man by whom the scandal cometh." The scandal of Judas did not destroy the Apostolic College; neither will scandals, how great soever they may be, destroy the work of the Almighty. The divine side of the Church will always remain pure and true like its Divine Author; the human side is subject to the weaknesses of our fallen human nature. "Thou art Peter, and upon this rock I will build my Church and the gates of hell shall not prevail against it." This suffices; Peter is still there, and shall abide there until the judgment day.

Years ago the following caricature fell under my eyes. It represented Bismarck and his imps holding a long cable, which was around the cupola of St. Peter's' and pulling it with all their might. Satan appears, crying out, "Hallo Bismarck! what are you doing?" "I want to pull down this Church," answered the Chancellor. "Bah! you waste your time," said the devil, "I have tried that job myself, these 1800 years, and have failed."

Returning to my mission, I imparted to my parishioners the blessing of the Pope, and continued my missionary work until a paralytic stroke rendered me an invalid. I was then ordered to leave my dear mission of Brownsville and make San Antonio my home for the future. Encouraged by the clergy and many of the laity, I wrote my Reminiscences with the authorization of my Superiors.

When you hear that I am dead, please pray for me. I must now prepare for the long voyage of Eternity.

INDEX.

PART I.
Texas and Louisiana.
PAGE.

CHAPTER I.—1852. Adieu to Belle France. Aspect of the Diocese of Galveston. My first trip. Penniless. General Chambers. "Liberty." Sour Lake. Prayer answered. Two nights in a box. Back to Galveston. Yellow Jack. Second Mission tour. Raw sweet potato for my supper. Jasper.................. 5

CHAPTER II.—Calcasieu. My Mustang. Mary comes to my Rescue. Lost in the pine-wood. In the nick of time. Laudanum did it. Drowned girl swallowed by an Alligator. Cow Boys. How I crossed bayous. From Mensa Episcopali to a kitchen. Third trip. Fifty baptisms in a small settlement. Rivers Calcasieu and Mermenteau. Indians................ 12

CHAPTER III.—An Ablegate sent by Pope Gregory XVI. A Protestant Doctor. Bayou Pierre. Shreveport. Eight Negroes hanged. Back to Galveston. Bishop Odin, Abbe Dubuis. Father Neraz.................. 23

CHAPTER IV.—Father Verdet, O. M. I. The ill-fated Nautilus. Nine Days Floating on a Door; Father Keralum, O. M. I., making a Coffin. Lost in the Chapparals. Dies of hunger. Remains found after ten years. My fourth tour. A Baptist Minister. Sour milk. How I paid my fare.................. 27

CHAPTER V.—San Antonio. The Mysteries of a Convent. The Girl is really dead. What was found under the Statue. Grasshoppers. Exorcism.................. 33

PART II.

Mexican Side of the Rio Grande.

CHAPTER I.—A Saint? The Whole Country Astir. Tatita the Impostor. A Sight. A dangerous interview. The Hypocrite tries to arouse the Multitude. The Mayor alarmed. Tumult. Armed protection necessary. Tatita killed. 43

CHAPTER II.—Leyes de Reforma. Exiles. The Bishop of San Luis Potosi. Mgr. Verea, Bishop of Monterey. Tu quoque Ramirez!!! A Bishop who never entered his Diocese. Sudden death. Buried on Sand-Hills. 50

CHAPTER III.—Between Two Fires. Bagdad. Oblate Fathers in Matamoros. A Hold-up. Quick Justice. Another Hold up. No money for you. Stage Robbery. Remarkable Conversions. 55

CHAPTER IV.—Raid on Bagdad. A Pandemonium. St. Joseph's Protection. Bagdad is fallen. Troubled times. Victoria. Oblate Fathers victims of the Revolution. Civil War in Matamoros. Fall of Maximilian. 60

PART III.

On the Texas Side of the Rio Grande.

CHAPTER I.—Bishop Odin. Difficulties about the Boundary Line. His Honor the Mayor. A Crust of bread. Physical aspect. Religious Ditto. Field of labor. First House of Worship. First Residence. 79

CHAPTER II.—From the Archives of the Vatican and Copenhagen. Interesting notes on America, Mexico and Texas. Correspondence between d'Alarconne and De la Harpe.... 91

CHAPTER III.—Cortina. Raid on Brownsville. Impromptu Army. Took to their heels. Captain W. G. Tobin. Col. Rip Ford. Cortina defeated. Three Men hanged. Looked upon as a Spy. A Lawyer without a license.... 97

CHAPTER IV.—A Funny Interview. What Chewing tobacco did. A Protestant's remarkable Conversion. A Baby baptized in the Nick of Time. General Banks wants to study Spanish. A Poor Man hanged. An agreeable surprise... 103

CHAPTER V.—Terrific cyclone. Convent destroyed. The sleeping Girl saved. Four thousand five hundred Dollars subscribed. An Impromptu Sermon. A Queer way of making Money. 111

CHAPTER VI.—Bishop Manucy. Reception. Sisters of Charity. Scribes and Pharisees. A Mob. The Bishop's Palm Sunday. His Good Friday.... 115

CHAPTER VII.—The Mule's Tail. Up to the hub. "Try, Try Again." "There She goes." Bishop hunting... 120

CHAPTER VIII.—Father Bretault. A Lesson in Astronomy. Rustic scenes. A Sight. 127

CHAPTER IX.—The Right Rev. Bishop P. Verdaguer. Revisiting the scenes of my younger days. Oh! Quam mutatus ab illo... 133

PART IV.

From Mexico to Rome.

CHAPTER I.—Apparition of Our Lady of Guadalupe. Authentic Documents. Aspect of the Miraculous Picture. 139

CHAPTER II.—Office approved by Benedict XIV. New Office approved by Leo XIII. Two Distiches by the Pope. Indian festivities. Maguey. Pulque. Mescal. 148

CHAPTER III.—Puebla on December 12. Splendid scenery. Misa de Aguinaldo. The Pastores 151

CHAPTER IV.—Cathedral of Puebla. The Venerable Palafox. Process of Canonization failed. 165

CHAPTER V.—City of Mexico. Arrival of the Monks. The Hand of God is there. Predictions. Protestantism a failure. Don Pancracio. 169

CHAPTER VI.—Rambles through the City. Religious aspect. On the road to Toluca. Grand scenery. The Passionists............. 177

CHAPTER VII.—Morelia. A remarkable episode. Pazcuaro. Indian work of art. A famous picture. The River Lerma. Lake Chapala. A fish story..... 181

CHAPTER VIII.—Guadalajara. Leon. A great painting. Guanajuato. Our Burros. The Valenciana Mine. Zacatecas............. 185

CHAPTER IX.—Back to the City of Mexico. Tula. At the station; *Maguey Tostado*. Marquez; *Pulque, Guayavas*. Queretero; *Opals*. Celaya; *Cajetas*. Irapuato; *Fresas*. Aguas Calientes; *Frutas*. Chihuahua; *Leche*. Arizona, California. 190

CHAPTER X.—Santa Fe. Archbishop Lamy. To Europe. Ditched. Niagara Falls. Across the Ocean. Brest. Terrific tempest. Grande Chartreuse...... 193

CHAPTER XI.—Lourdes. Fr. Domenech. Cardinal Langenieux. She was cured. Power of Mary. Protestant lady cured and converted. Marseilles. ... 199

CHAPTER XII.—Loretto. A soldier says Mass. History of the Translation of the Holy House. Proofs of the Miracle. ... 204

CHAPTER XIII.—Rome. First Impressions. The Quirinal. My Cicerone. The Obelisk. Fontana. The Colonnade. St. Peter's Church. Michael Angelo. The Cupola. The Confession. ... 209

CHAPTER XIV.—The Vatican. The Mamertine Prison. The Catacombs. St. Stanislaus Kotzka. Montorio. The Pincio. St. Peter and St. Paul. Separation. ... 215

CHAPTER XV.—St. John Lateran. The Scala Santa. St. Mary Major. St. Paul. St. Benedict Labre. Holy Cross of Jerusalem. Domine Quo Vadis? St. Peter's Chains. ... 219

CHAPTER XVI.—In Rome, the stones speak. Audience of the Pope. Pause. The Gates of Hell shall not prevail. ... 223

THE MAVERICK

THE POPULAR HOTEL OF SAN ANTONIO.

AMERICAN AND EUROPEAN PLANS.   CAFE ALWAYS OPEN.

THE MOST CONVENIENT HOUSE IN THE CITY
ALL CAR LINES PASS THE DOORS.

M. A. WEBB.

LARGE, LIGHT SAMPLE ROOMS.

Johnson Bros. Printing Co.

308-310-312 Navarro Street.

..PRINTING..
BOOK BINDING.

Lowest Prices
Best Work.....

SAN ANTONIO, TEXAS.

This Book was Printed and Bound by us.

MENGER HOTEL, SAN ANTONIO, TEXAS.

H. D. KAMPMANN, PROPRIETOR.   M'LEAN & MUDGE, MANAGERS.

MENGER HOTEL

... SAN ANTONIO ...

First-Class in All Appointments.

BEXAR HOTEL

First-Class Family Hotel.

TERMS REASONABLE.   EXCELLENT TABLE.

BOOKS
AND
STATIONERY.

SCHOOL BOOKS
AND
SCHOOL SUPPLIES.

COMMERCIAL PRINTING.

Lowest Prices.
Prompt and Careful Service.

320 W. Commerce St.
San Antonio, Texas.

NIC. TENGG,
Bookseller, Stationer and Commercial Printer.

I Carry a Line of.. ..

Religious Articles,

Rosaries, Crucifixes, Statuary, Holy Water Founts, Medals, Scapulars, Candlesticks, Etc.

Prayer Books,

In English, German, Spanish and Polish, various Binding, Sizes and Print, at all Prices.

NIC. TENGG.

"Reminiscences" FOR SALE BY NIC. TENGG, SAN ANTONIO, TEXAS.

ACADEMY OF OUR LADY OF THE LAKE, San Antonio, Texas. (For Particulars Apply to the Mother Superior.)

The Goggan Piano

EMBRACES everything that a thirty-two years' experience with the Texas climate would suggest, and for the price and terms it is sold on it has no superior and we doubt if an equal. In tone, finish and quality it is fully warranted, and we back the instrument with our reputation. Besides the Goggan we still handle and carry in stock ten distinct makes of Pianos in different styles, including the world's leaders. We sell them as low and on as easy payments as they can be purchased anywhere. Don't pay commission agents, strangers and and half-profit men $400 and $500 for unknown boxes, when you can get a standard, first grade Piano for that money. Parties selling goods on commission or on half the profits have uo regular price for the boxes they sell; the more they get the more profit there is to divide. Purchasers of Pianos would do well to hesitate before placing their orders for unknown makes of Pianos with strangers, commission agents and half-profit men. We handle the world's best productions in Pianos, and we also handle the cheapest Pianos made, but remember we warrant everything we sell and can always be found to make our warranty good. You run no risk in buying a Piano of us. We will give you better value for your money than you can get anywhere and sell you on easy payments WITHOUT NOTES.

THOS. GOGGAN & BROS.

www.ingramcontent.com/pod-product-compliance
Lightning Source LLC
Chambersburg PA
CBHW021804230426
43669CB00008B/623